Simple Signing with Young Children

A Guide for Infant, Toddler, and Preschool Teachers

Carol Garboden Murray

Acknowledgments

A special thanks to the children, teachers, and students at the Dutchess Community College Child Care Center in Poughkeepsie, New York, for modeling the signs in this book.

Dedication

This book is dedicated to Charlotte Jean Garboden.

Special Thanks

The publisher would like to thank Gryphon House employee Kerry Sweeney and his family for sharing their extensive knowledge of American Sign Language with the author and editors of this book.

Simple Signing

with Young Children

A Guide
for Infant, Toddler, and
Preschool
Teachers

Carol Garboden Murray

gryphon house

Beltsville, MD

© 2007 Carol Garboden Murray
Printed in the United States of America.

Published by Gryphon House, Inc.
10726 Tucker Street, Beltsville, MD 20705
301.595.9500; 301.595.0051 (fax); 800.638.0928 (toll-free)

Visit us on the web at www.ghbooks.com

Photographs by Paul Rich
Cover Photograph: Straight Shots

Library of Congress Cataloging-in-Publication Data

Murray, Carol Garboden.
 Simple signing with young children / Carol Garboden Murray ; photographs
by Paul Rich.
     p. cm.
 Includes bibliographical references and indexes.
 ISBN-13: 978-0-87659-033-1
 ISBN-10: 0-87659-033-4
 1. American Sign Language--Study and teaching (Early childhood) 2.
Nonverbal communication in education. I. Title.
 HV2474.M87 2007
 419'.7--dc22
                     2006035415

 Gryphon House is a member of the Green Press Initiative, a nonprofit program dedicated to supporting publishers in their efforts to reduce their use of fiber sourced forests. For further information visit www.greenpressinitiative.org

Bulk purchase
Gryphon House books are available for special premiums and sales promotions as well as for fund-raising use. Special editions or book excerpts also can be created to specification. For details, contact the Director of Marketing at Gryphon House.

Disclaimer
Gryphon House, Inc. and the author cannot be held responsible for damage, mishap, or injury incurred during the use of or because of activities in this book. Appropriate and reasonable caution and adult supervision of children involved in activities and corresponding to the age and capability of each child involved, is recommended at all times. Do not leave children unattended at any time. Observe safety and caution at all times.

Every effort has been made to locate copyright and permission information.

Table of Contents

Preface

Every now and then, something comes to us in our profession that revitalizes our practice. For me, these gifts arrive in various forms: an amazing book, an inspiring colleague, a unique child. Sign language has been one of these gifts, and that is why I am so happy to share *Simple Signing with Young Children* with you.

This book emerges from my 18 years of teaching in early intervention programs, special education classrooms, integrated preschools, nursery schools, and community childcare centers. In each of these different educational environments, children have responded enthusiastically to communicating through sign language.

I first learned to use a few key signs in the classroom while teaching hearing children with learning disabilities, including children with Down's syndrome and autism. Later, while teaching in integrated settings, I found that all children were motivated by signs and loved talking with their hands. Creative storytelling has always been an important part of my teaching practice, and I discovered signs are a great way to be more expressive, make stories come alive, and invite children to interact during literacy activities. Inspired by sign language, I developed a sign-and-sing story hour for children in my community, held at a local family network center. When my first son was born, I used signs with him starting at about eight months of age. My heart leapt when he signed back to me for the first time. There is nothing quite so moving or that will make you appreciate the beauty of sign language as much as having a preverbal baby communicate with you through sign. When my second son was born, I formed a signing playgroup to teach other parents the joys of early communication through sign language.

When we teach children to sign, they can see, feel, and hear language. It is children's natural inquisitiveness that motivates them to learn this new code. Sign language is a natural tool for boosting a child's self-esteem and engagement. Children who have a hard time following verbal directions will find something to hold on to and something to look at. These are tools they will need to become more successful and independent. Children who have difficulty expressing emotions or reading social cues will benefit from this immediate, hands-on means of expression. While I was teaching a small group of children with Pervasive Developmental Disorder, I learned that sign language is a great way to create a common classroom language for children who speak languages other than English, as one of my students spoke Japanese in the home and another other spoke Arabic.

Sign language is an effective classroom management tool that allows you to create a peaceful classroom environment. Not only can sign language benefit young children, but it also can make you a more artful and sensitive teacher.

Most importantly, we know that the key to quality early education lies in trustful relationships, and sign language is an elegant way to make connections. My hope is that this book will enhance the good work you do each day with young children, and will help you create a unique relationship with the children you teach.

Carol Garboden Murray

Carol Garboden Murray

1

Introduction to
Using Sign Language with Young Children

A three-year-old child practices the sign for *open*.

American Sign Language: Am I Learning a New Language?

Although the use of sign language with hearing children is growing in popularity and is more commonly accepted in the mainstream, misconceptions still exist about how it works. Many teachers feel overwhelmed by the idea of learning or teaching a new language, but there is no need to feel intimidated. This book demonstrates how easy it is to use a sign vocabulary. You may start by choosing one or two key signs and, for the most part, use the signs along with the spoken word. The American Sign Language (ASL) vocabulary you use will be a tool for many things, such as reinforcing language learning, assisting with classroom management, fostering prosocial behavior in young children, and promoting early literacy skills.

This book will not teach you to be fluent in ASL, but it will help you use sign vocabulary that is meaningful to you and the children you teach. Like any language, ASL is complex. A common misconception is that ASL is a signed version of English and that if you possess a sign vocabulary you can simply translate English into sign, word for word. This is not true because ASL, like all languages, has its own grammar and syntax. The only way to become fluent is to study the language and spend time with others who are fluent. Proficiency in sign language goes far beyond building a vocabulary.

Yet, once you learn a sign vocabulary that is meaningful to your relationship with children and your teaching practice, you may be inspired to learn more about ASL. Similarly, learning signs may help children connect with others who use ASL fluently or it may spark their interest in learning more about this expressive language. The beauty and power of speaking with your hands may inspire you as a teacher to take a class, purchase a good ASL dictionary, or invite ASL-fluent guests into your classroom.

ASL uses handshapes, facial expression, location, and movement to represent words, ideas, and concepts. It is the language used by over 500,000 deaf people in the United States and Canada.

The popularity of ASL has increased tremendously in the past decade. Many colleges offer ASL as a second language elective. Parents are learning about the benefits of using sign language with preverbal babies as a way to foster language and decrease frustration. Special education teachers and teachers of hearing children are experiencing the benefits of using sign language in the classroom. It is estimated that 13 million people can sign with some level of proficiency. This makes ASL the third most commonly used language in the United States.

How Will I Teach Hearing Children About ASL?

Teaching ASL vocabulary to hearing children introduces them to another culture and can potentially expand their appreciation and acceptance of a diverse world. Members of the deaf culture advocate an accurate understanding of ASL as a distinct and dynamic language. Hopefully, as more educators and young children enjoy the benefits of ASL, they will also promote a respect and appreciation for the language.

About This Book

Simple Signing with Young Children presents the basic skills for understanding and using an ASL vocabulary as well as practical suggestions for incorporating ASL into the classroom. Of course, for babies (and toddlers), you do not need to explain to the children why you are using ASL. Use signs that are meaningfully embedded in your day, and they will become for the children a natural form of communication alongside the spoken word.

With preschoolers, it is great to jump right in, too. Start using a few signs in your daily routine to allow children some time to become accustomed to seeing you use signs before needing to explain too much about what you are doing. Around age three or four, children are ready to learn about ASL. As you incorporate more signs into your teaching practice, answer questions and present information respectfully and accurately. There are developmentally appropriate suggestions for teaching hearing children about ASL and the deaf culture in the preschool chapter (Chapter 5).

This book demonstrates how you can use a sign vocabulary every day. The photographs in the book show ASL's immediate application for the important work you do with babies, toddlers, or preschoolers. How you use signs with young children emerges naturally from your relationship with the children you teach, and it depends on the age group you are working with as well as your goals as a teacher. Some teachers may start by using just two or three basic signs with infants and toddlers during this exciting period of language acquisition. Even a few signs, such as *more* and *all done,* can be a significant help in creating a peaceful group setting and reducing frustration for preverbal children. Other teachers may choose to incorporate signs more completely into the daily routine and use signs to give children directions at clean-up time and group time (without needing to call across a busy room).

This book focuses on many different ways to incorporate sign language into your curriculum. Chapter 2 introduces techniques for using sign language as a tool for classroom management and enhancing children's social skills. Chapters 3, 4, and 5 discuss using sign language with children of different ages. Chapter 6 examines how to modify the techniques for inclusive classrooms. The classroom management chapter is a good place to begin because it includes universally relevant and easy-to-apply suggestions. Also, the letter to parents at the end of each chapter includes helpful information to share with families.

Your approach to ASL in the classroom will be slightly different for babies, toddlers, and preschoolers. Chapters 3, 4, and 5 address these differences. Chapter 3, Sign Language for Babies, focuses on using beginning signs as a bridge to language, while Chapter 4, Sign Language for Toddlers, focuses on using signs with toddlers to promote expression, enrich vocabulary, and teach social skills. Chapter 5, Sign Language for Preschoolers, places an emphasis on using signs to enhance emergent literacy skills.

Use the index to find specific signs. Although the chapters are divided by age groups, many signs are appropriate for all age groups. For example, beginning signs such as *more* and *all done,* found in the baby chapter, are also appropriate for toddlers and preschoolers.

Although there are many ways to use sign language with children between the ages six months and five years, the common theme throughout this book is relationships— better communication between you and the children to strengthen your relationship with them.

Tips for Using Signs with Young Children

- **Use signs during meaningful interactions.** Start with signs for words you use as you interact with children during your daily classroom routine. The classroom management chapter contains several signs that are easy and meaningful to put into practice with your children.

- **Start simply.** When you introduce signing into your classroom, begin with two or three signs. For babies and toddlers, you can start with the signs *more* and *all done*. For preschoolers, start with classroom management signs or signs you can use in songs or stories. Let your experience using signs grow with the children's enthusiasm.

- **Be consistent.** Once you start using a few signs, be consistent and practice using those signs all day long. Repetition is key!

- **Be expressive.** Facial expression is an important element of ASL. A good signer communicates with her whole being. Sign language is much more than practicing handshapes. Have fun!

- **Use resources.** Have several resources available, including this book, other teacher guides, and an ASL dictionary. If you have access to the Internet in your classroom, refer to an online dictionary such as the American Sign Language Browser by Michigan State University Communication Technology Laboratory (http://commtechlab.msu.edu/sites/aslweb/browser.htm). Having resources available allows you to relax and take risks. If a child asks you how to make a certain sign, you can let her help you look it up. Remember, it is okay to make mistakes, and using resources like dictionaries with the children helps foster the sense that they are in a community of learners.

Embed a sign vocabulary within your daily activities and routines to improve communication with young children. The possibilities are endless and will emerge naturally from your practice. Using a sign vocabulary allows you to:

- teach babies to express themselves before they are able to speak;
- improve vocabulary and communication with babies and toddlers;
- help toddlers practice emerging social skills;
- reduce frustration for late talkers;
- reach children with special needs;
- introduce young children to ASL and the deaf culture;
- create a common classroom language for children who speak other languages;
- enhance songs and fingerplays;

- increase attention and engagement;
- increase children's sense of accomplishment, mastery, and self-esteem;
- foster emergent literacy skills;
- create a more peaceful classroom; and
- improve your creative storytelling.

Variation in Signs

As you learn signs and use dictionaries and sign language resources, you will discover variations for certain words and phrases. Try to remain open and flexible, realizing that language is dynamic and always subject to a variety of interpretations, pronunciations, or regional differences. Cross-checking a few references will help you decide which sign is more common. Talking to fluent signers is always the best resource to help you understand subtleties or regional differences.

Practicing Handshapes

ASL uses handshapes to express words and concepts. Learning the ASL alphabet is a good way to practice handshapes. Here are some common handshapes.

Flat Hand (fingers together)

Open Hand (fingers apart)

Curved Hand

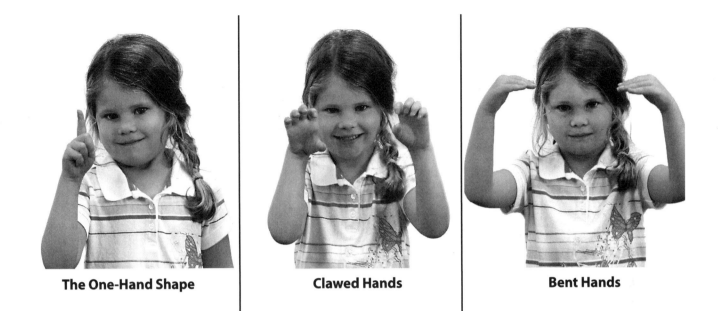

The One-Hand Shape   **Clawed Hands**   **Bent Hands**

Practice the following signs with the above handshapes:

Flat Hand

Fish: Use the flat hand to make a fish swimming in front of your chest.

Thank you: Use the flat hand extending from your chin or mouth as if blowing a kiss.

Open Hand

Mommy: Open fingers wide and place your thumb on your chin to sign *mom*.

Daddy: Use the *open* hand and place your thumb near your forehead to sign *dad*.

Curved Hand

The Letter C: The curved hand naturally forms the letter C.

Drink: The C handshape represents a cup as you mimic drinking.

Elephant: The C handshape at your nose mimics an elephant trunk as your arm extends.

One Hand

Go: Use both hands with one finger extended, bend at the wrist to point *go*.

Up: Use one hand to point *up*.

Clawed Hand

Hot: Abruptly pull your clawed hand away from your mouth to represent *burning* or *hot*.

Bear: Cross your clawed hand in front of your body and move your body in scratching motion.

Bent Hand

Blocks: With hands facing, bent hand touches the wrist of the other flat hand.
Duck: Make the bill of a duck with a bent hand and place it at your mouth.

Facial Expressions

Facial expressions are key components of strong communication skills. When you sign it is important to be animated and expressive. Signing appeals to children because they love drama and pretend play.

Happy   Lion

Expression is particularly important when signing emotions. Imagine happiness bubbling up as your flat hands tap your chest in circular motions.

A four-year-old child pretends to be a lion as he produces the sign by making the lion's mane.

The Dominant Hand

Those fluent in ASL use their dominant hand as they sign, and they use this hand for all one-handed signs. Most ASL dictionaries and guides show right-hand dominance. Practice to see which hand you are most comfortable using, and use this hand as your primary signing hand. You may notice that young children alternate hands and sometimes use both hands. Just as we appreciate babbling, word play, and mispronunciation with language in the early years, we should also be flexible with the way children use signs. Model and teach ASL accurately, but allow for experimentation and encourage risk-taking as children learn to sign. When working with babies and young children, sign with the hand you have available. Don't let a busy hand keep you from signing!

Bird   Cat

Only one hand is used to sign *bird*.

Although only one hand is used to sign *cat*, children often do this sign with two hands—as they visualize making a cat's whiskers on their cheeks.

Location

ASL uses location to express words and concepts. For example, male signs are always made near the top half of the face (near the forehead to symbolize wearing a hat), while female signs are always made near the bottom half of the face (near the chin to symbolize the strings of a bonnet tied around the chin).

Daddy   ## Mommy

With an open hand, use your thumb to tap your forehead and wiggle your fingers slightly.

With an open hand, use your thumb to tap your chin and wiggle your fingers slightly.

Movement, Action, and Mimic

ASL also uses movement to express words and concepts. Sometimes when you sign with movement, it feels or looks as if you are acting out the word. For example, the sign for *stop* (see below) is a sign that uses movement. It is a logical sign, because the movement of the sign—bringing one hand downward with the other hand stopping it abruptly—"feels" like the word.

Stop: Children feel the word *stop* as one hand chops down abruptly on the other hand.

Banana: Children visualize a banana as one hand acts out peeling the pointer finger (the banana).

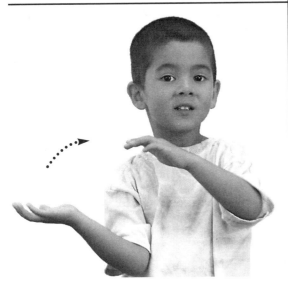

Wind: Children imagine a windy day as the hands sway back and forth to show the movement of the wind.

Some signs are symmetrical. They require identical movement of both hands.

Play	**Shoes**
Make the Y handshape with both hands and shake your hands back and forth.	Form two shoes with your closed fists and tap them together several times.

Using the Signs in This Book

Iconic Signs

One of the great things about ASL is that many of the signs are iconic, meaning they actually look like the word. These visual cues make it easy for children to learn and remember language. For example, to sign *eat,* you touch your fingertips to your lips. To sign *moon,* you make a crescent near your eye. There are many iconic signs that are fun to use in stories and songs at group time and throughout the day within classroom rituals and routines.

Functional Signs

Functional signs are often wonderful classroom management tools, and children can use them in social situations. The most common functional signs for young children to use are *more* and *all done.* Other helpful and common functional signs are *pain, help, please, thank you, yes,* and *no.*

Pain (Headache)

Pointer fingers quickly touch each other to indicate pain. The sign for *pain* is a directional sign—the location is important and changes. If your head hurts, the sign is made on your head. If your knee hurts, the sign is made on your knee.

Action Signs

Action signs such as *sit, stop, go, slow, fast, wait, jump*, and *dance* are appropriate to teach and use while playing games, dancing, and listening to music. These signs are also helpful management tools. Use them to give children directions, such as "sit down," "stop," or "slow down." Children feel empowered if they learn to sign *stop* to assert themselves in social situations that might be emotionally charged and might otherwise end in hitting or pushing.

Emotions Signs

The signs for emotions are easy to teach during a song, such as, "If You're Happy and You Know It." It is helpful to use emotion signs when coaching children through social exchanges or conflicts. When using sign language, and especially when using signs to indicate emotions, be sure to use corresponding facial expressions. These signs are great to use in the classroom because they help children tune in to the feelings of others, read facial cues, and express themselves.

Signs for Daily Routines

Teaching signs for the activities of daily living helps you communicate with the children in your classroom throughout the day. These signs are particularly helpful during transitions and when giving directions to children about the schedule, what time it is (for example, snack time) and what's coming next (for example, music).

Toys and Classroom Center Signs

Copy the signs for common toys and classroom centers and post them with the written labels so children can learn them.

People Signs

Children enjoy learning the signs for *mommy* and *daddy*. Teaching children the signs for *children, boy, girl, friend,* and *teacher* is also helpful. These signs can be used during classroom transitions and routines. ("It's time for to *girls* to line up." Thank you, *children*.")

Nature, Seasons, and Animal Signs

Children enjoy learning animal signs, and story time offers a perfect opportunity to teach these signs in a meaningful way. Signs give children a new way to interact with books and stories. You can also teach them some nature and season signs to use during songs and fingerplays or while teaching them about the weather or changing seasons.

Concepts

Teachers can reinforce the meaning of concepts by using signs. Signs for prepositions like *in* and *out* are iconic—thus making meaning very concrete for young children. Children enjoy learning the signs for colors and playing color games using signs.

In summary, remember that one of the great benefits of working with young children is the opportunity to learn and grow right along with them. Keep your resources handy and approach learning signs with the openness of a child. Let the children be your inspiration to jump in, experiment, and have fun!

2

Using Sign Language to

Manage the Classroom and Teach Social Skills

A three-year-old child practices the *stop* sign.

Sign language helps teachers become more creative and reflective. It demonstrates how communication is a complex system that includes words, gestures, tones, volume, movement, and expressions. When you use signs, you pay closer attention to what you say and how you say it.

Sign Language for Daily Routines

Sign language is most meaningful to young children when you embed signs within the daily schedule and routines. Functional activities such as snack time, clean-up time, and the various transitions throughout the day hold just as many valuable lessons as the more explicit teaching opportunities at group time or project time.

Using signs for classroom management adds a new dimension of learning to daily activities. Children learn signs effortlessly when you use them as a classroom management tool because signing becomes a part of the communication system in the classroom community. Using signs to help children learn social skills is motivating and powerful for young children, because it is closely linked to a purposeful emotional experience.

Sign language helps children learn social skills. Signing can emphasize appropriate social conventions, such as when to say, "Please," "Thank you," and "I'm sorry." Signs can validate children's emotions and help them tune in to the emotions of others. Sign language can be a powerful tool for children to express their boundaries and reduce frustration; for example, when they learn to use the signs for *stop* or *help*.

A child signs "Thank you."

Signs such as *my turn* and *your turn* can help teach basic social skills during play. Sign language also provides another way to praise children, facilitate gentle guidance, and support children's sense of well-being and belonging in the group setting. Ultimately, sign language enhances your relationships with children and their relationships with one another because it improves everyone's ability to communicate.

Sign Language to Enhance Classroom Management

Thank You/Good

Thank you can be used silently (without words) for nonverbal praise, or it can be used with the words as a model and as reinforcement. *Thank you* is a very helpful sign to use during social coaching and as a prompt during snack and meal times. Signing courtesy words such as *please* and *thank you* gives the words special emphasis, thus reinforcing the value placed on kindness in the classroom.

Hand starts at lips and moves outward, as if blowing a kiss (this sign means both *good* and *thank you*).

Modeling *sorry* throughout the day as you work with the children in social situations offers another way to accentuate empathy and coach children during meaningful interactions with their peers. When teaching this sign to very young children, it is helpful to knock on your chest lightly with the *S* hand (hand making the handshape for the letter *S*) as you move it in a circular motion. This is a good way to help children distinguish *sorry* from *please* (because both signs move in circular motions on the chest).

Sorry

Place an *S* hand on your chest and move it in a circular motion.

Model signing *please* throughout the day as you talk to other teachers and to the children. You can prompt children to say "please" by using the sign. It is a subtle way to remind children to use their manners without having to say, "What's the magic word?" It is not appropriate to withhold an object a child wants until the child makes the *please* sign, but it is always supportive to offer a friendly model.

Please

Place a flat hand on your chest. Rub chest in a circular motion (as if to warm your heart).

Sign Language to Support Positive Social Behavior

Share

When you use this sign, imagine slicing a cake or dividing food to share with others. The movement of the hand represents dividing things up. Both hands are flat and open with fingers together.

Friends/Friendship

When you use this sign, imagine two people hugging and being close friends. Bring your index fingers together and interlock them several times.

Gentle Touch

Use the gentle touch sign while coaching children to be gentle with one another. **Note: This is the ASL sign for *slow***—it is modified here for young children who benefit from the immediate visual and tactile feedback of this simple gesture of one hand petting the other.

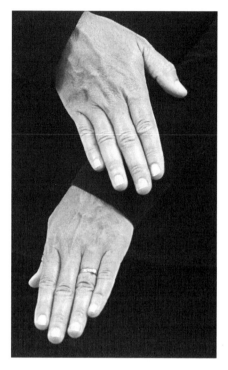

"One hand pets the other."

Gentle

With palms up, open and close your hands in a gentle way.

Touch

Use middle finger to touch back of other hand.

My Turn, Your Turn

These signs are essential for anyone working with young children. Put them into action immediately while playing with children and facilitating appropriate social exchanges.

My

Using a flat hand with your fingers together, touch your chest to indicate *my*.

Your/Yours

Using a flat hand with your fingers together, move your hand forward to indicate *your*.

Help is a powerful and useful sign. Use the sign when saying, "We need some *help* cleaning up the toys," or "Thank you for *help*ing." Teach the *help* sign when a child shows frustration and needs to learn to ask for assistance. Toddlers will shriek, point, and grunt when then need help opening a package, operating a toy, reaching a desired object, or negotiating an obstacle. To reinforce the sign, use it when saying, "You look like you need some *help*" or "You can say, '*Help* me, please.'"

Help

The fist of one hand rests in the palm of the other hand. Lift hands up together several inches in front of your chest. Imagine one hand "helping" the other hand up.

Sign Language to Help Children Learn Impulse Control

Throughout the toddler and preschool years, children are learning to control their impulses. Hands are the tools of learning as well as natural tools for expression. That's why it's so natural for children to grab, push, and hit when they are frustrated rather than use language to solve problems. Putting language in the children's hands by teaching them to use the *stop* sign during social conflicts is a perfect way to encourage them to use their hands in conscientious and appropriate ways. Children really like to do this sign because it makes them feel powerful.

Stop and Go

Teachers and parents often encourage children to use their words when coaching appropriate social behavior. However, this is an abstract request for many young children and can be frustrating for them when they aren't able to retrieve the words they need. Teaching children to use the *stop* sign reduces their frustration in emotionally heightened social situations. This useful sign gives children's hands something important to do, and naturally diverts those hands from the impulse to hit or push. The stop sign is also perfect for children who may be more passive and need to learn to assert or protect themselves. Quiet children respond well to this concrete way of expressing their boundaries.

Stop

Before age two, children typically bring hands abruptly together to produce the *stop* sign. By age two, children begin to position the base hand flat against the edge of the other hand.

Chop down quickly with your action hand into a flat base hand. Imagine something coming to an abrupt stop.

A 17-month-old child doing the *stop* sign brings his hands together quickly.

Go

Several variations exist for the *go* sign in different ASL dictionaries. This simple version is the best for children.

Point your index fingers and make a swift movement forward as if to indicate, "Go."

Play "Stop and Go" Games to Practice Self-Control

To reinforce the signs for *stop* and *go* with the children, play modulation games. This type of play is also great for developing children's self-control.

Recite the following rhyme with the children and use the stop sign when you say the word "stop."

Shake, shake, shake my sillies out, and now it's time to stop.
Jump, jump, jump my wiggles out, and now it's time to stop.
Twirl, twirl, twirl my giggles out, and now it's time to stop.

Other ways to reinforce these signs include the following:
- Play music and encourage the children to sign *stop* when the music is off and *go* when the music is on. Use the signs to encourage the children to do the appropriate action.
- Lead a "stop-and-go march" around the room and use the signs to tell the children what to do.

Fast and Slow

Try using the signs *fast* and *slow* while playing "Stop and Go" games to further reinforce modulation and control. For example, use *stop* and *go* signs to have the children jump fast and slow, spin fast and slow, shake the parachute fast and slow, and walk on tiptoes fast and slow. This is fun to do silently. Children must pay attention to your sign to know which way to move.

Fast

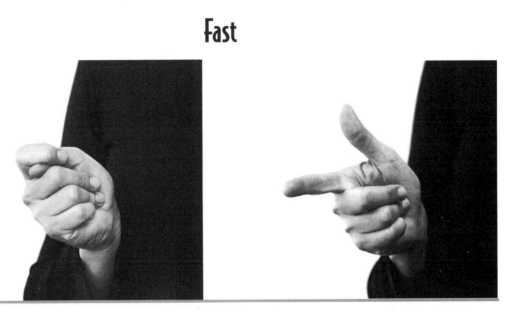

Tuck your thumb under your index finger, and then quickly snap it
out to show something moving quickly.

Slow

Draw one hand slowly up the back of your other hand.

Sign Language to Help Children Express Emotions and Read the Emotions of Others

Social coaching is the perfect time to use signs for encouraging children to express their emotions. While helping a child negotiate a compromise or resolve a conflict, validate his strong emotions by using signs with facial expressions. In these situations the child can literally see the word *angry* or *happy* and see his emotion reflected in your face as he produces the sign—what validation!

Some children find social interaction difficult and have a hard time reading subtle cues (facial expressions) from their peers. Using sign language helps children tune in to the emotions of other children. Signs reflect and validate emotions.

Use signs for emotions during social coaching. You validate children's emotions when you use signs that show how they feel.

- "I see you are *sad*."
- "It made you *angry* when he took that from you."

Help children see the power and consequences of their behavior by using signs to show them how they impact others.

- "He looks *happy* because you gave him a turn!"
- "He is *crying* because you took the toy from his hand."

Sad

Move outstretched fingers down your face to represent sad feelings or tears.

Angry

Move clawed hands up toward your face. Think of rage rising up inside you.

Happy

Pat your chest and move in circular motions with flat hands.
Imagine happy feelings bubbling up.

Cry

With your fingers, show tears rolling down your cheeks.

Sign Language to Help Ease Transitions

Transitions can be difficult and confusing for children. Using consistent visual and auditory cues helps prepare children for change and eases the transition period. During transitions, use signs while giving directions as a way of presenting the message visually as well as orally. Transitions can also be a great time to use signs without any words. Sending a silent message during a busy active period is a perfect way to communicate peacefully. Management tools such as the "Two More Minutes" song (see page 42), the *all done* sign (see page 44), and *one more time* sign (see page 43) give children warnings, help children receive and register a message, and give children some control over their environment through consistent and clear communication.

Quiet

Start with one finger at your lips to indicate *quiet*.

Calm

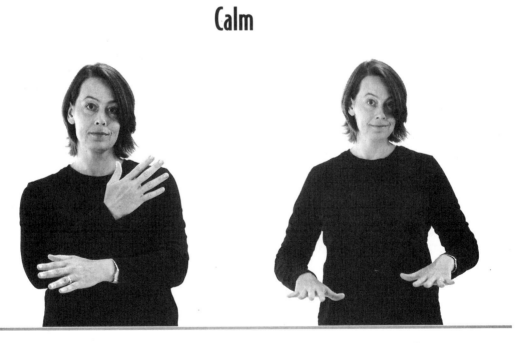

After making the *quiet* sign above, cross your arms and sweep them down in a smooth, graceful motion.

Cleaning

Move one hand in a circular motion as if cleaning the surface of the other hand.

Time

Point to your wrist as if checking the time on your watch.

Get

Your

Reach out your hands as if to get something and bring them to your chest.

Using a flat hand with your fingers together, move your hand forward to indicate *your*.

Coats

Imagine pulling a coat over your shoulders.

Line Up

Point your fingers up straight (with thumbs tucked in) to represent people standing in line. Start with your hands a few inches apart and move them away from one another to show a line forming.

Walk

Place your flat hands in front of your chest with palms facing down. Move your hands forward alternately as if to symbolize the walking motion of feet.

Sit

Include the *sit* sign while reciting this rhyme with the children.

One, two, three, four, _____ (child's name) is sitting on the floor.
One, two, three, four, _____ (another child's name) is sitting on the floor.

Keep chanting the rhyme and adding the names of all the children as they join you.

Use two fingers of one hand to "sit" on two fingers of the other hand
(imagine legs sitting on a bench).

Two More Minutes

When it is time to clean up, try giving a quick environmental cue such as turning the lights on and off quickly or ringing some chimes. Then sing the following song, including signs when appropriate, and encourage the children to join you in singing. Children often pause to put down their toys because they need to use their hands to sing and sign. Even if some of the children don't sign along, they receive a consistent visual and pleasant auditory cue that prepares them for the upcoming transition.

Two More Minutes

(Sung to the tune of "Happy Birthday to You")

Two more minutes to play.
Two more minutes to play.
Two more minutes,
Two more minutes,
Two more minutes to play.

Two Hold two fingers up.

More Tap your fingertips together.

Minutes Hold one hand flat like the face of a clock. Move the index finger of your other hand in an arc to indicate minutes ticking.

To Touch your index fingers together.

Play Make Y shapes with each hand and pivot them back and forth at the wrists.

One More Time

When children engage in repetitive play, use this phrase with signs to help them prepare for the activity to end.

One

More

Bring your hands together and tap fingers together repeatedly.

Time

Draw one hand slowly up the back of your other hand.

All Done/Finished

All done is a sign that you can use throughout the day. Toddlers respond especially well to this sign, and it helps children accept closure of an activity. Children will represent this sign in different ways. Some children will flip their wrists and twist their hands back and forth. Others will open and close their hands swiftly, while still others will simply make a forward sweeping motion or side-to-side motion as if to push something away.

Start with your palms facing up and then flip your hands outward.
Imagine clearing the table.

Sign Language to Help Children Pay Attention

Sign language keeps children's attention because it provides them with visual and kinesthetic cues, enabling them to follow directions and be more successful in group settings.

Using signs to give directions, such as *stop, look*, and *listen,* makes directions less intrusive. To enhance children's language acquisition, it is good to use sign language with spoken words. However, occasionally use it silently. Sign language allows you to send and receive messages from across the room without raising your voice.

Children respond well to sign language because seeing a sign and knowing what to do without being "told" promotes independence in children. Sign language allows you to give quiet prompts, thus modeling calm behavior and facilitating children's independence.

Stop

Chop down quickly with your action hand into a flat base hand.

Look

Use a *V* hand to represent the eyes looking forward.

Listen

Cup your hand to your ear.

Ready

Use the *ready* sign at the beginning of group time to get everyone's attention. After the children learn its meaning, do the sign quietly and watch to see how many children catch on and begin to do it with you. Children like the idea that they understand a secret code and know what to do without being "told." You can acknowledge the ones who begin to do it with smiles and nonverbal praise, and before you know it, you'll have everyone rocking from side to side with the *ready* sign. Keep the novelty of this sign by using it sparingly, but keep it in your transition repertoire.

With two *R* hands (cross your first two fingers), point out to one side. Swing your hands from side to side.

Know

Know is a helpful sign to use during group discussions or group time. When posing a question, encourage the children to indicate that they know the answer by signing *know*. This helps children develop some impulse control, allowing them time to think about what they know before waving their hand in the air or calling out the answer.

Touch your fingertips to your forehead.

Wait/Waiting

Use *wait* during group time to encourage children to be patient when they have to wait for a turn. Children can learn to be comfortable with quiet wait time and not jump in and answer for one another. You can help children become accustomed to wait time by using this sign to build pauses into group time.

With palms up, wiggle the fingers of both hands.

Thinking

Try adding the sign for *thinking* to group discussions:

- "Let's *wait*, someone is *thinking*."
- "I'm *thinking* about it."
- "Let's all *think* about this story. If you could be an animal, what animal would you be?"

Touch the middle of your forehead with your index finger. Move your finger in small circles in front of your forehead, as though to indicate gears turning.

Remember

Remember is a word that comes up quite often during group discussion. Signing *remember* visually acknowledges thinking about something (as you touch your forehead), and it contributes to creating a moment of contemplation, inviting everyone to think about the question you've just posed.

Try incorporating the *remember* sign as you say the following:
- "Do you *remember* the names of the characters in this story?"
- "Who *remembers* the story we read yesterday during story time?"
- "*Good* work, you *remembered* the sign. I see you're *ready*!"

Touch your thumb to your forehead, and then touch it to other thumb
(as if to know something and to keep it).

Yes and No

Teach the children to use the *yes* and *no* signs to answer questions during group time. This is a great way to allow everyone to answer at the same time!

Yes

Shake an S hand up and down. Imagine a head nodding, "Yes."

No

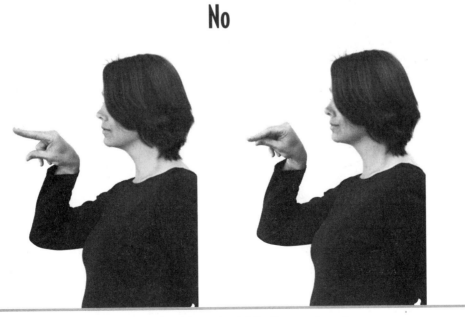

Snap your thumb and middle finger closed.

Signs You Can Use to Praise Children

Smart

Touch your middle finger to your forehead.

Clever/Smart

Touch your index finger to your forehead and then move it away from your head
as you point forward. Imagine forward thinking.

Good Work

Good

Start with a flat hand at your lips and move it outward, as if blowing a kiss
(this sign means both *good* and *thank you*).

Work

Use one *S* hand to tap the other *S* hand, as though hammering.

Idea

Try signing, "Good idea," with the children.

Bounce your pinky finger off your forehead, then move your hand up and out
from the side of your head.

Girls and Boys

The sign for *girl* originates from a time when girls wore bonnets.

Try signing, "Smart girl" or "Smart boy."

Use the *girl* and *boy* signs with transitional phrases:
- "All the *girls* can line up."
- "One, two, three, four, the *boys* are sitting on the floor."

Girl   Boy

With an *A* hand, stroke the side of your cheek   Bend your hand at your forehead as if
or chin along the jaw line.   touching the rim of a cap.

Try signing, "Good choice," with the children.

Choice

Use one hand to pick and choose from the fingertips of the other hand.
Envision picking berries.

Perfect

Touch a *P* hand to the other *P* hand.

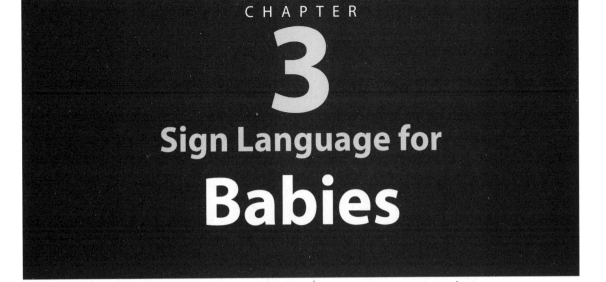

CHAPTER

3

Sign Language for

Babies

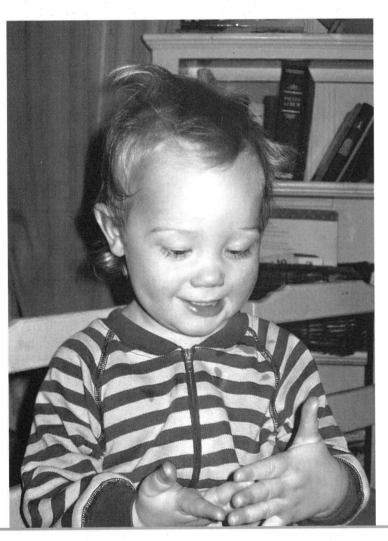

A 13-month-old child produces the sign for *book*.

Infants Learn Signs Through Interactions

Whether you are changing a diaper, reading a book, or teaching a child a new word or sign, you are doing invaluable work. There is no hierarchy in the importance of the caring and teaching tasks you perform each day, which makes it easy to incorporate signing into the daily routine of caring for and teaching babies. Start simply, with words and activities you already use frequently. Adding a sign will enhance the experience for both you and the children. Sign language validates the work of early childhood educators because it accentuates the importance of your interactions with babies. The daily care you give babies during meals, diapering, and dressing is the best place to start using signs because it is in these caregiving rituals that relationships and trust form.

The most important thing to remember is that language develops through interaction. If you believe that relationships are the key to quality care and you enjoy face-to-face interactions with babies during diaper time, book time, and play time, then you already have the foundation you need to incorporate signing into your daily routine.

Research on Signing with Babies

Joseph Garcia, author of *Sign with Your Baby*, and Linda Acredolo and Susan Goodwyn, authors of *Baby Signs*, are the pioneers of signing with hearing babies. Joseph Garcia became fascinated with the idea of signing to babies while working with the deaf culture in the late 1980s. He noticed that babies of deaf parents used gestures and signs to communicate with their parents several months before hearing babies started using vocalizations and words to communicate. He hypothesized that hearing babies could learn to communicate earlier (with signs) before they have the oral motor skills to produce words. With the help of the 17 families in his study, he learned that babies who are exposed to signs regularly and consistently at six to seven months of age can begin using signs by eight to nine months.

Linda Acredolo discovered "baby signs" after observing her 12-month-old daughter spontaneously inventing gestures. She created a series of *Baby Signs* books and videos to teach parents how to communicate with their preverbal children. With her colleague, Susan Goodwyn, Acredolo proved through compelling research that babies who learn signs have greater vocabularies at age two and actually have increased IQs (by 12 points) at age eight. The research supported what baby signers witnessed all along—signing doesn't keep babies from talking; it actually helps them learn how to talk and improves vocabulary and IQ scores.

Benefits of Signing with Babies

Babies who sign can communicate before they can speak. Babies acquire the ability to understand language long before they have the oral motor skills to produce words. All the skills necessary to say words are very intricate and complex. Signing can bridge the gap between comprehension (understanding language) and expression (speaking).

Babies who sign experience less frustration. When a baby has a way to express her needs and wants, there is less opportunity for frustration to set in. Babies soon discover that signing is more satisfying and productive than crying or grunting and pointing.

Babies who sign develop larger vocabularies in the early stages of language acquisition. Research proves that by age two, signing children have 50 more words than those who don't use sign language. Signing is a pathway to language.

Babies who sign can also experience a close bond with their caregivers. The real reason to encourage signing is to support relationships through successful communication!

Baby signing *airplane* with a teacher.

Signs Help Caregivers Understand Babies' Needs

One of the wonderful things about using signs with babies is that it gives caregivers a peek into babies' minds. Anyone who cares for babies feels the joy of connecting with such fresh, young spirits. As you tune in to a baby's personality, you can quickly anticipate her needs. As you speak to a baby, her responses show how she is beginning to understand language. There's nothing more exciting than seeing the spark in a baby's eye as she uses her first sign and shows you what you know—she has something important to say!

In addition to all the benefits signing offers, one of the reasons it makes sense to use signs with babies is because it is natural for children to use their hands to communicate. Once babies discover their hands, they begin to raise their arms to be picked up, to reach for objects, to push things away, and to point to objects to show you what they want or what they are interested in. Signing is just one way to capitalize on what babies do naturally before they have the necessary oral motor skills to produce words and communicate in sentences.

Babies and adults always use gestures and body language to communicate with one another. When you point, nod, use exaggerated facial expressions, and respond appropriately to a baby's gestures, you are communicating. Signing goes even further by giving specific symbols to key words, reducing the potential for frustration and taking some of the guessing game out of communication.

Why Use Baby Signs?

For the most part, you can model and use ASL as you sign with babies. ASL is a beautifully expressive language and a wonderful tool. However, you do not need to learn ASL fluently, nor do you always need to use ASL to use sign language as a tool for communication with babies. You only need to learn key signs and use a sign vocabulary in conjunction with speech. The primary reasons for signing with babies is to communicate with them and to promote their language development. You want babies to hear, see, and feel the sign. Helping babies to communicate through signing is the first step in helping them to talk.

It is good to be flexible and allow for a few invented baby signs, though most of the time it is best to use ASL. As you think of a sign you want to use with a baby, look it up in this book or in an ASL dictionary. Use ASL as much as possible because, as you do, you create a common language in your classroom for children, teachers, and parents. Also, using ASL allows consistency for babies in several environments. ASL is growing in popularity among teachers of hearing children, so babies may be in a position to continue to learn ASL as they grow into toddlers and preschoolers, at which time they will already have a foundation for learning. But, sometimes using improvised or "baby sign" is a better choice than ASL when working with babies. Below are a few situations where you might consider using a baby sign rather than ASL.

Babies Will Not Sign Perfectly

Because you are using sign language to teach babies how to communicate, you must consider how babies learn language. Babies don't start talking by saying words perfectly—they babble, play with sounds, and produce partial words. Signing is similar. When signing with babies, be flexible, allow for variation, and celebrate the wonderful things babies do with their hands, faces, and bodies to communicate. For example, *water* is signed by placing a *W* handshape at your lips. Babies do not have the coordination to make the *W* shape. They usually take one finger and touch their bottom lip with it to imitate this sign. These baby signs should be encouraged as babies experiment with sign language.

The ASL Sign for *Bottle*

The *bottle* sign in ASL is abstract and often hard for babies to create. However, giving babies the tool to ask for a bottle early on is important because it is often a baby's first sign. You may notice that "baba" or some similar word approximation is often an early and important word to babies. To make a sign that babies can understand, sign *bottle* by putting your thumb to your mouth as if sucking a bottle. This is the same sign used in the book *Baby Signs* by Linda Acredolo and Susan Goodwyn. (In the case of *bottle*, it is typical for babies to stop using the sign as soon as they can say "bottle" or "baba," because the word is more immediate and powerful. Many similar baby signs will fade as babies master words.)

Generalizing Signs for Babies

Sometimes, try generalizing signs for babies rather than always using accurate ASL. Doing so resembles baby talk. For example, some teachers will choose to use the sign *bed* (head resting on your hand) to mean several things such as *sleep*, *tired*, *nap*, and "*night-night*." Similarly, the sign *drink* might mean water, juice, milk, and so on. This is appropriate because these signs are bridges to language. Generalizing and simplifying signs for babies is similar to the baby talk you naturally engage in when working with infants.

Babies Invent Signs

Sometimes babies invent their own signs for favorite objects, and it is worthwhile to consider using these with the babies. Think of it as celebrating the baby talk stage. When a baby invents a sign, she is indicating an understanding of symbols and has the right underpinning to become a successful communicator. For example, my first baby began signing in the summer. At the time, garden hoses fascinated him. One day he made up a sign for *hose* by pointing his finger and making a hissing sound. We used this sign together and it worked wonderfully! Later, I looked up the sign for *hose* and learned that, like most water signs, it uses a W handshape that is too difficult for a 13-month-old child to reproduce. So, we continued to use my baby's sign instead: he could already perform the sign, and we understood one another perfectly.

When Are Babies Ready to Learn to Sign?

At ages as young as six and seven months, babies are ready to focus on signs. When they can begin to support themselves and are learning to sit up, it's a great time to begin to use a few signs as you talk with them. Babies may start signing back as early as nine to 10 months, although many babies do not start using signs until they are about 12 months old. Because each child develops at a different pace, it's more important to look for milestones than to count months. Here are a few key milestones that usually occur between six and 12 months to watch for as you sign with babies:

- Babies discover their hands.
- Babies drop toys and look for them.
- Babies seem to understand a few words.
- Babies point.

Babies Discover Their Hands

Before babies begin making their first signs, you may notice them watching you and paying more attention to your hands. They may want to touch your fingers and may reach for your hands as you sign.

A significant milestone is when babies start gazing at their own hands, opening and closing their fingers, and attempting to put their hands together. Although babies may not be making signs at this point, they start to pay closer attention and discover their own tools for communication. They are making progress toward being physically able to sign.

As you care for babies, observe how they discover their hands. This is a good time to document progress for each baby and share these exciting milestones with parents:

- The baby gazes at her own hands.
- The baby opens and closes her fingers.
- The baby puts her hands together.
- The baby claps.
- The baby transfers an object from one hand to the other.
- The baby reaches for adults.
- The baby reaches for objects.
- The baby pushes objects away to show she is not interested.
- The baby points at objects.

Babies Drop Toys and Look for Them

Object permanence is an important milestone because it shows that babies have the ability for symbolic thinking. By dropping a toy and then looking for it, a baby is indicating that she can imagine the object exists even when it is out of view. This skill is linked to memory. Babies need to have memory and the ability to hold images in their minds before they can start signing. Babies start to develop these thinking skills by the time they are six months old.

Babies Seem to Understand a Few Words

Babies let us know through their eye contact and body language that they understand words. For example: when a baby looks up to you with a special awareness, anticipation, and intelligence, you can see that she knows what you are talking about. When you say another person's name, the baby looks to that person. When you mention that it is time to go outside, she looks towards the door. When babies have these symbols in their heads, but they do not have the oral motor skills to produce the words, it's the perfect time to begin using signs. It not only gives them visual symbols for the words (as they watch you repeat the word and the sign together), it will soon give them the ability to communicate with their hands!

Babies Point

Some babies start pointing at objects as early as eight months. Most master pointing and do so in a deliberate and determined way by 12–14 months. Pointing is an amazing early accomplishment that is easy to take for granted because it is such a natural part of our daily communication system. When you understand how complex the act of pointing is, you can see how closely it is related to communication and language.

Pointing is symbolic. In doing so, the baby makes an imaginary line, connecting the object in the distance to the end of her finger. She also trusts that those with whom she hopes to communicate can do the same.

Pointing is an invitation to communicate and a way for a baby to show she understands that communication is about connecting with another person. It's the baby's first way of saying, "Look what I see—share it with me!"

Pointing shows us that a baby has a developing self-concept. To point out objects, a baby must understand that she is an individual, occupying her own space, separate from you.

Pointing to objects is the precursor to labeling objects. As a baby points, she begins to create a visual library of all the objects in the world by pointing to them and noticing that one object is different from another. A baby can use pointing to collect knowledge, asking adults to teach her the words that match all the things she is noticing in her ever-expanding world.

Are Your Hands Full?

During your daily caregiving routine, your hands are very full! It is beneficial to use correct ASL whenever possible, but there are times when you may need to improvise. Rarely will you have both hands free and a baby sitting right in front of you with undivided attention, so it is important to be flexible and to use signs as much as you can, however you can. At this stage it is more important to be repetitive (do signs as much as possible) than perfectly accurate.

For example, when using signs while reading a storybook, you might find yourself signing in the book rather than right in front of your body. If the baby is looking at a picture of a cat, you might find yourself using your fingers to make the *cat* sign (pretending to smooth the whiskers with two fingers) right on the picture of the cat, and then as the baby shows interest, you might sign *cat* on the baby's face. Another time, when the baby is looking right at you, you'll have the perfect opportunity to sign *cat* on your own face.

It is best to make the *thank you* sign with your dominant hand, but because it comes up often and deserves constant reinforcement, simply sign *thank you* with whichever hand is most readily available. If both hands are full, consider ask an older toddler to do the sign for you. This works for many signs; for example, "Ben, will you show Anna how to make the sign *more*. She looks like she really wants to say 'more' and my hands are full!"

Tips for Getting Started

- **Start simply.** Start with two or three words you use all day, such as *more* and *all done*. Next, choose words that represent the baby's most pressing needs, such as *eat*, *milk*, or *bottle*.
- **Be consistent and repetitive.** Babies need to see and hear a sign many times before they will produce the sign themselves.
- **Use the repetition within the daily routine to create meaning.** When the baby is eating, sign *eat*. When the baby is looking at a book, sign *book*. When you put music on, sign *music*.

- **Speak when you sign.** Emphasize the word as you sign it, point to the object, and make the sign. Do all these things to help babies make the connection between symbols and objects.
- **Sign favorite objects.** After you are comfortable using a few beginning signs, notice the things that the baby looks at or wants all the time. Learn the sign for those favorite objects, such as *light*, *ball*, *dog*, or *car*.
- **Be patient.** When babies aren't yet signing back to you, keep signing (remember, repetition is key). The younger the baby, the longer it will take. When babies do start signing, you will feel affirmed and motivated.

More Ideas for Teaching and Reinforcing Signs with Babies

Hand over Hand

The hand-over-hand approach can be very meaningful because it helps a baby feel the sign. You most likely already practice this technique. For example, if you take a baby's hand to help her wave goodbye before she has learned to do this by herself, you are already using the technique. Always do hand over hand gently and only when the baby is receptive, never forcing her.

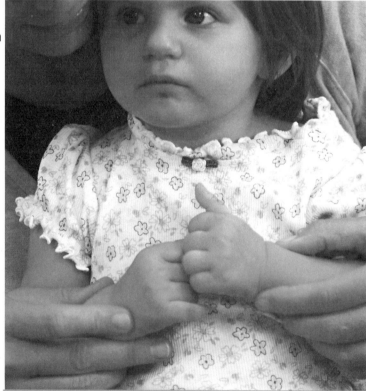

A teacher uses the hand-over-hand technique, helping the child produce the sign *more* by bringing her hands together.

Point to Objects

Pointing to objects and pictures of objects in books is a way to teach differentiation of objects and help babies expand their vocabularies. It is a way to show them that pointing is a means of communication and encourage them to use their hands to communicate with you. When signing a favorite object, say the word, make the sign, and point to the object as a way of reinforcing the connection between words and objects.

Praise and Acceptance

Greet all forms of a baby's nonverbal and gestural communication with enthusiasm and warmth. A baby can understand the subtleties of nonverbal communication very early in life. She can tell by reading her caregiver's facial response and eye contact if her communication attempts are received or rejected.

Signing on a Baby's Body

Using your own hands or fingers on a baby's body is another way to reinforce a sign. For example, when signing animals, play with signs as you talk with the baby. You might make whiskers on her face while talking about cats, or touch her nose while talking about elephants.

Signing in Books

Although it is best to sign when a baby is looking at you, this becomes complicated when she is focused on a picture or a book. Signing on a picture or a book is a fun way to reinforce a sign. It also reinforces the iconic nature of signs and helps the baby develop symbolic thinking.

A teacher produces an animal sign on the book by using her fingers to smooth the whiskers of the kitten illustration.

Beginning Signs

Before a baby can speak, she can communicate her needs by gesturing, gazing with her eyes, using facial expressions, kicking her feet and waving her arms when she is happy, or throwing things or pushing things away when she is upset. Two basic needs she communicates first are "more" ("I like that," "I want more of that," "That makes me happy," "Give it to me!") and "all done" or "finished" ("No thanks," "I'm done with that," "Stop," "I don't like it," "Take it away."). Learn these two signs and use them consistently throughout the day. These two beginning signs will satisfy more needs when communicating with preverbal babies.

Natural Opportunities to Teach Beginning Signs

More

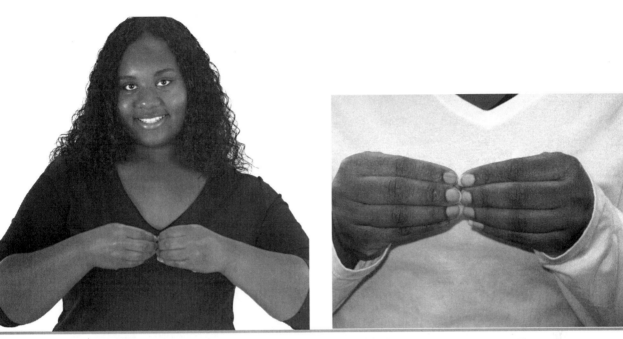

Bring your hands together and gently tap your fingers together repeatedly.

Meals. When you are feeding a baby and she looks to you with her mouth open to indicate she wants more, say, "Oh, you want *more*," while signing *more*. If the baby isn't looking at you, but is looking at the baby food jar or box of crackers, you can do the sign right on the food or in front of the food as you say, "more." You can also use the *more* sign if you give a baby a few small pieces of food to feed to herself. She may eat them quickly and reach for the box to indicate she wants more. To practice signing *more*, give the baby just two or three bites of food, so that you'll have the chance to repeatedly sign *more*.

Play time. During novel or engaging activities, such as when you blow bubbles, babies watch with interest, kicking their legs and laughing. When you stop, they kick their legs frantically to indicate they are waiting for more.

When doing repetitive baby games, such as stacking objects, hand the toys to the baby for her to stack them one at a time. After giving her one object, pause until she makes eye contact with you, indicating that she wants more. Repetitive games, such as stacking or putting toys in and taking them out of containers, are great opportunities for reinforcing the *more* sign. Similarly, when playing physical and repetitive baby games, such as "peek-a-boo," pause occasionally so the baby will look at you in anticipation, then sign and say, "Oh, you want *more*" before continuing the game.

All Done/Finished

Move open hands outward as if finished with something or pushing something away.

Meals. When you feed a baby and she turns her head away to indicate she is done, say and sign to her, "I see you are *all done*."

Play time. When you push a baby on a swing and she tugs on the swing and whines to indicate she wants out, stop the swing, then say and sign *all done*.

Transitions. When play time is over, begin to put the toys away. When a baby looks to you to see what you are doing, say and sign, "We are *all done* with toys."

Closure. As you finish changing a baby's diaper, say and sign, "Now we are *all done* with diapers." This can help a baby learn to wait for your signal, and not struggle during diaper change.

Common Ways for Babies to Reproduce Signs

More

Although some babies tap their fingers together to produce the sign *more*, many babies will produce slightly different variations of the sign. Some babies will knock their knuckles together, while other babies may tap the fingers of one hand into the palm of the other, or even just use one finger to tap into the palm of the other hand.

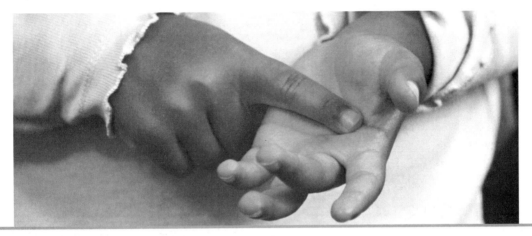

Baby pointing to hand to sign *more*.

Generalizing "More" to Mean Many Things

"More" is usually the first sign babies and toddlers produce. They get a lot of reinforcement when they sign "more" and get "more" of what they desire. Often, babies will generalize this sign once they've found it to be successful. They will use the sign "more" for everything (every time they want to communicate). This is similar to generalizations that babies make when they are learning to talk. For example, a baby will learn the word "dog" and will call all animals "dog." After practicing the new word or sign, they will begin to differentiate. Generalization is a normal process in language development.

All Done or Finished

Although some babies will be able to rotate their wrists to imitate *all done*, here are some other common ways babies sign *all done*:

- Flapping their hands in front of them.
- Pushing their hands toward you.
- Opening and closing their hands several times.
- Swinging their hands from side to side.

Signs for the Daily Routine

Now that you are using the signs *more* and *all done* throughout the day, begin adding other signs within your daily routine. Using signs throughout the day is great because they are meaningful to the children. The repetition also provides practice. Babies need to see and hear the sign over and over before they will produce it. Children thrive when they have an environment that provides predictability. Using signs within the daily routine adds another level of predictability for babies, thus fostering their feelings of security and safety while they are in your care. The rest of this chapter presents the most popular signs to use with babies throughout the day. These signs will also serve to strengthen the baby's vocabulary and help her express her needs when she begins signing back to you. See Chapter 4 for more meal-time signs, such as *cookie*, *cracker*, *apple*, and *banana*. Also see Chapter 4 for *thank you* and *please* signs, which are appropriate to use at meal time as well.

Meal-Time Signs

Eat

More Meal-Time Signs

Thank you, see page 25

Please, see page 26

Cookie, see page 108

Cracker, see page 109

Apple, see page 107

Banana, see page 108

Tap your fingertips to lips as if eating.

Drink

It is good to use the signs *eat* and *drink* often, particularly at meal and snack times. Say and sign, "Do you want *more* to *eat*?" to the children. With drinks, consider using the sign *drink* to represent all drinks, or use specific signs, such as *bottle*, *juice*, *milk*, and *water*.

Cup a hand at your mouth and tip your head up as if drinking from a cup.

Water

Water is a sign that comes up often, not only in terms of drinking, but because many babies love playing in water during baths and water play. Babies will typically modify this sign by putting one finger on their lips.

Put a *W* hand to your lips.

ASL Bottle

Adapted Sign for Bottle
(used by babies)

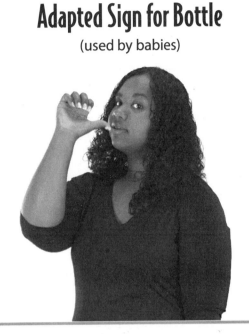

Imagine you are grasping the bottle with one hand and placing it on the other hand.

Use your thumb or finger to symbolize a bottle. Mimic a drinking motion with this adapted sign.

Milk

Open and close your hand repeatedly as if milking a cow.

Up and Down

Using signs with babies is simple and natural. Babies and adults have always used gestures to communicate with one another. Using the signs for *up* and *down* is a wonderful way to teach the basics of communication—it is the first step to help a baby understand that her needs can be met through gestures.

Up

When a baby reaches out to be picked up, pause for a brief moment to say and sign, "You want *up*," and then pick the baby up.

Down

When a baby indicates she wants to get down from a high chair or swing, pause for a brief moment to say and sign, "You want *down*," and then help the baby down.

Nap Time Signs

Many teachers choose to use the *bed* sign as a generalized sign. You may choose to sign either *sleep* or *bed* as you say "nap time," "sleepy," "tired," or "night-night."

Sleep

Sweep an open hand down over your face and close it near your chin.

Bed

Rest your head on your hand.

Tired

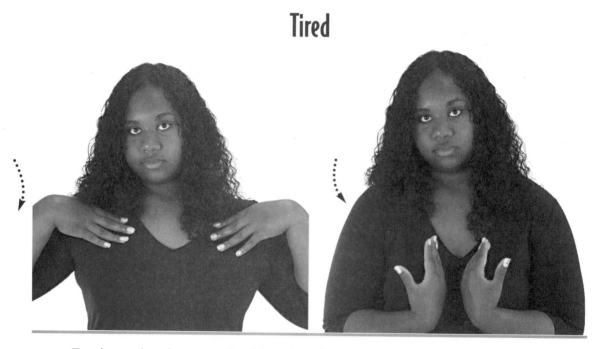

Touch your hands to your shoulders, then droop as you hunch shoulders forward.

Blanket

Pull your hands upward from your waist, as if pulling a blanket up over you and tucking yourself in.

Diaper Change Signs

Using a sign for *diaper change* or *toilet* will give you and the children a consistent way to indicate that it is time for a change. As the baby moves into toddlerhood, she will be able to use this sign to tell you she needs a change. The sign you use is up to you. You may find it easiest to just sign *change* (rather than *diaper change*). You might also use the sign for *toilet* so that the meaning will be consistent when children begin potty training.

Diaper

Hold both hands up as if pinching the corners of a diaper.

Toilet

Shake a *T* handshape slightly from side to side.

Change

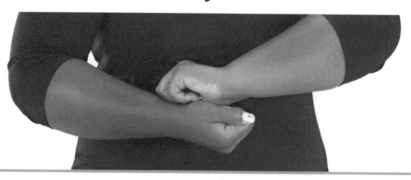

Rotate fists back and forth as if shifting/changing.

Favorite Things Signs

As you use signs within your daily routine, begin to add the signs for the common things you touch and play with every day, such as a baby's favorite toy. Playing with, looking at, pointing out, and talking about favorite items are natural opportunities to add to your sign vocabulary.

Car/Truck

Rotate hands as if driving.

Ball

Form a ball shape with your fingers, as if grasping a ball with your palms facing.

Baby

Sway your arms together as if rocking a baby.

Train

With palms facing down, slide first two fingers of one hand (*U* handshape) forward
and back along the first two fingers of the other hand.

Signs for Things That Are Way Up High

There are always special things that catch a baby's eye, and babies often look up and notice things above them, such as Mylar balloons in the grocery store, fans on the ceiling, and airplanes in the sky. Here are some of the signs for things many babies take interest in and like to point to.

Fan

Point your index finger up and circle it around to mimic the fan spinning.

Balloon

Hands begin close to the mouth. Move hands outward as if holding a balloon while blowing it up.

Light

With one hand, point closed fingers down, then spread your fingers as if
rays of light are shining down.

Airplane

The shape of your hand represents an airplane flying overhead. The hand is in the *I Love You*
position. This is difficult for children under age three to do. Infants and toddlers will use an
open hand or pointer finger flying overhead.

Moon

The C handshape represents a crescent-shaped moon.

Pain, Hurt, or Ouch!

Although most babies will not start using the sign for *pain* until they are 12 months old, it is an important sign to teach early. This sign can be an invaluable tool one day when a baby has an earache and can actually tell you she is in pain!

It is helpful to get into the habit of signing *pain* to the children. You can sign it each time a baby bumps her head, for example, as a way to validate her experience: "*Ouch—that hurt!*"

Pain

Pain is a directional sign. So, if your ear hurts, you should make the sign near your ear. If your knee hurts, make the sign near your knee. If babies like to sing "Five Little Monkeys Jumping on the Bed," you can pause after a monkey bumps its head and say, "Ouch!" while making the *pain* sign.

Touch your fingertips together quickly on your forehead to sign *headache*.

Signs Are Like Pictures

These favorite baby signs are iconic—the baby is able to show or act out the word.
Here are some signs that are iconic (other signs are on pages 72 and 73).

Bird

Form a beak with your hand in front of your lips. Open and close thumb and finger to
show a beak opening and closing.

Fish

With your fingers together, "swim" your hand in front of you like a fish in water.

Book

Open and close your hands in front of you as if opening a book.

Singing with Signs

Songs and chants are a perfect medium for helping babies develop vocabulary and strong language skills. It's easy to understand, therefore, how songs can be a useful way to practice and reinforce signs as well. If you enjoy singing with babies, you can add signs to songs within the daily routine.

Sing the following verses with the children to the tune of "Here We Go Round the Mulberry Bush," making the appropriate signs.

This is the way we take a bath... (scrub body up and down with closed hands)

This is the way we brush our teeth... (move finger back and forth in front of teeth)

This is the way we eat our snack... (sign *eat*)

This is the way we read a book... (sign *book*)

Did You Hear That?

When babies start tuning in to environmental sounds, such as the telephone ringing or the knock at the door, they will often look to an adult as if to say, "Did you hear that?" This is a perfect time to encourage them to use signs to communicate. Simply point to your ear or cup your hand around your ear to indicate that you heard the sound. Soon, the baby will also begin pointing to her ear to indicate that she hears something.

Listen/Hear

Cup a C handshape around your ear.

Sound

Point to your ear.

Music

Sweep a flat hand up and down the other arm rhythmically.

Auditory Discrimination

When babies respond to environmental sounds, comment on the sounds and make the accompanying signs as a way to reinforce language, auditory discrimination, and symbolic thinking or visualizing something unseen.

Telephone

Hold your hand up as if talking on the phone.

Siren

Lift claw handshapes overhead while rotating at the wrists to show lights spinning on top of an ambulance.

Signing with Books

Goodnight Moon by Margaret Wise Brown

Goodnight Moon is a great book to sign with babies, because you can show each picture and then make the corresponding sign on the page. Don't be overwhelmed by signing every item as you read, however. Focus on pointing to and identifying objects and making a game of signing the babies' favorite objects.

Because some copies of *Goodnight Moon* are small and difficult to sign on, make a large version of the room in the book on a piece of poster board so that you can sign the names of the objects right in front of the board. Babies will love looking at the room and pointing to the items. It makes signing easier also, because you are not focused on turning pages and signing at the same time.

It is also fun to replicate the items in the book (balloon, light, kitten, mitten) with large pieces of felt on felt board. This is a great way to make the story come alive for babies and to play with words and signs.

Signs to Use in Goodnight Moon:

Moon Make a C handshape near side of forehead.

Balloon Hands begin close to mouth. Move hands outward as if blowing up a balloon.

Light Begin with closed fingers pointing down. Open up fingers as if light is shining.

Telephone Use your thumb and pinky finger to form a telephone.

Socks Rub your index fingers back and forth against each other.

Clocks Point to your wrist as if looking at the time.

House Outline the roof of a house with your hands.

Mouse Brush your index finger on your nose to indicate twitching nose of mouse.

Kittens Smooth out the whiskers of a cat on your cheeks. **Note:** This is the ASL sign for *cat*. Use the sign for *baby* (p. 82) and *cat* to say *kitten*.

Signs to Use in **Goodnight Moon:**

Mittens Mimic action of putting on mittens.

Cows Make an *L* handshape with hands and put them on your head to show horns of a cow.

Jump With two fingers of one hand, act out jumping in the palm of your other hand.

Bears With arms crossed, use clawed hands to open and close fingers as if to scratch.

Chairs Show the *sit* sign and repeat it. Sit: place two fingers of one hand on two fingers of your other hand.

Brush Mimic holding brush and sweep hand downward as if brushing.

Bowl of Mush Use your hand to mimic eating cereal from a bowl.

Old Cup chin with your hand an move downward to show a long beard.

Lady Use the thumb of your shaped hand to stroke your cheek near the chin. Tap your chest with the thumb.

Letter to Families

Dear Families:

In our classroom, we are using an American Sign Language vocabulary for key words as we care for and play with babies.

The exciting thing about using signs is that it helps us improve our relationships with the babies we care for. Being able to communicate with one another better and sooner makes everyone happy.

We speak as we sign, emphasizing key words. Signing is a way of connecting words to movement and visual symbols. Signing and speaking together helps the baby see, hear, and feel the words. This multisensory approach stimulates communication pathways in the brain, making it easier for babies to learn to talk. The benefit of signing with babies has been well documented through research.*

If you wish to learn more about the benefits of using sign language, or if you have any questions, please feel free to ask.

Sincerely,

Babies who use signs:

- can communicate before they have the oral motor skills to speak.
- are less frustrated.
- experience closer bonds with caregivers.
- develop larger vocabulary and language skills.
- have more active imaginations.
- develop a greater interest in pictures and books.
- have higher IQs.

*From a comparison study by Susan Goodwyn, Ph.D., and Linda Acredolo, Ph.D., of the University of California at Davis. The study compared signers and nonsigners at ages two, three, and four, and then measured their IQ scores at age eight.

4

Sign Language for

Toddlers

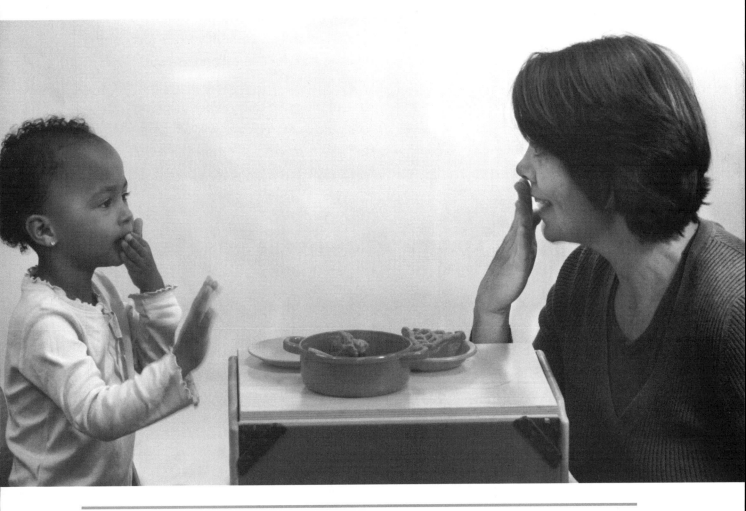

A teacher signs *thanks* to a toddler while playing.

Using Sign Language with Toddlers

Teaching signs to toddlers is like giving them a gift—a little bag of tricks for expressing themselves during this exciting stage of life. This chapter presents signs that are particularly popular with toddlers.

Beginning Signs Build a Foundation

Just as with babies, you will want to sign with toddlers throughout the day, creating meaningful interactions during meal time, play time, and nap time. If you are just getting started with toddlers, review Chapter 3 (Sign Language for Babies) and use the beginning signs such as *more* and *all done* in your daily routines. All the information in Chapter 3 is applicable to toddlers as well. One of the great things about signing with toddlers is that they will sign back much more quickly than babies will, which is motivation to keep signing. If you are working with a mixed age group, the toddlers can help reinforce signs for the babies. They love to show the younger ones the skills they master.

Signs Improve Communication for Late and Early Talkers

Communication skills develop at vastly different rates for each child. Signs can be a bridge to words for late talkers. During toddlerhood, it can take many months for children to properly articulate words, so it is common to misunderstand early talkers. Combining signs with words can help clarify what children are trying to say. When toddlers use signs and words, it reduces the guessing game that sometimes accompanies early conversations between you and toddlers.

Screenings, Evaluations, and Early Intervention

Although it is important to appreciate the differences and variability within speech/language development, it is critical not to overlook a child who may need speech/language therapy early on. Screenings for toddlers help determine if a child should be referred for an evaluation. Your local early intervention agency is a valuable resource for working with children from birth to age three.

Signs Tap into the Child's Desire to Move

The toddler world is all about movement, and signs allow children to express themselves with their bodies. It's very physically satisfying to make signs. Even toddlers who are quite advanced talkers will find gratification through signs, especially in emotionally charged situations when language is harder to access.

Signs Promote Confidence

Signing gives children a sense of confidence because it is something toddlers can do well. Signs promote a child's sense of self during this important time of self-discovery.

Signs Reduce Frustration

Between the ages of 12 and 35 months, sign language has enormous potential for reducing the communication frustration that toddlers may feel. This is the age when children start using words, but they also use other sounds, such as grunts and cries to express wants, needs, or protests when they can't find the words to express what they want and need.

When a toddler grunts and points at an object, you can say, "Oh, you want the ball," while simultaneously using the signs *want* and *ball*. Using signs to respond to grunting, pointing, and whining will help toddlers learn to use these signs as tools for appropriate expression. Signs are much more effective and specific than grunts.

Negative Emotions and Temper Tantrums

Although some sign language books and programs claim that signs will eliminate toddler temper tantrums, signs shouldn't be used for that goal exclusively. In appreciation of this time of life when children are developing their individuality and autonomy, it is important for children to experiment with limits and power and words like "no" and "mine." Healthy environments for young children allow expression of the range of positive and negative human emotion. When a toddler screams in frustration because someone took his toy, you can help him say "mine" or "that made you angry" by signing and giving him validation as well as an immediate tool for expressing himself. Your goal is not to eliminate his strong emotions, but rather to validate his feelings and give him an appropriate way to express his feelings. You are saying, "It's okay to be angry—and here's a suggestion for what you can do when you feel such a strong emotion."

Signs for Pretend Play

Toddlers are just beginning to use their symbolic thinking skills to represent their world through play. They love imitating adult roles, such as talking on the phone, cooking, and taking care of babies in the dramatic play corner. Use pretend play as an opportunity to sign. Use signs to ask your toddler's favorite stuffed animal if it wants *more* to eat, and then offer it some pretend food while smacking your lips. This type of activity reinforces representational skills by teaching the toddler to sign as well as encouraging his understanding of objects and signs as symbols.

A teacher signs *more* during pretend play.

Beginning Signs for Toddlers

Review Chapters 2 and 3 to learn basic signs such as *more, all done, help,* and *stop.* Use the beginning signs *more* and *all done* throughout your daily routines with toddlers.

Functional Signs for Toddlers

Once toddlers are using a few signs to make their needs known for food, drinks, or favorite items, start using the *want* sign. For example, try signing, "want more" or "want milk please" at meal time. Other functional signs include *open/close, hot/cold, pain/ouch.*

Want

Extend both hands out and then bring them closer into the body while the fingers curl up.

Toddlers may simply open and close fingers to show the sign.

Toddlers sometimes pull their fists right into their chests.

Beginning Signs

More, see pages 43 and 69

All done, see pages 44 and 70

Help, see page 29

Stop, see page 19

Open and Close

Open is a sign that comes up frequently with toddlers. Doors and latches fascinate toddlers, and they often like to play open-and-close games. *Open* also comes up when toddlers need help opening containers.

Open

Move flat hands apart as if opening a window.

Close

Move flat hands back together. Toddlers may represent this sign by placing their hands flat together and then opening and closing them like a book.

Social Signs for Toddlers

Review Chapter 2 and Chapter 3 for important social signs such as *stop*, *gentle touch*, *please*, *thank you*, *sorry*, *my turn*, and *share*.

When sharing information with families about the use of social signs with toddlers, it is often fun to teach them how to sign *I love you*. Practice this sign while singing songs about love with the children, such as "Skidamarink" (see Chapter 5). Parents and children enjoy knowing this silent code, which gives them a special way of saying "I love you" from across the room. Toddlers will generally hug themselves to show the *love* sign. For the ASL sign *I love you*, see Chapter 5 (Sign Language for Preschoolers). For other emotion signs, see Chapter 5.

Love

Important Signs for Toddlers

Stop, see page 31

Gentle touch, see page 28

Please, see page 26

Thank you, see page 25

Sorry, see page 26

My turn, see page 29

Share, see page 27

A toddler signs *love* by crossing her arms in front of her chest as if to give a hug.

Safety Signs

Important safety signs for toddlers also include *stop*, *look*, and *listen* (see Chapter 2).

Cold

With closed fists, shiver as if you are cold.

Hot

Place a cupped hand to your mouth and quickly draw it away as if your breath is hot.

Pain/Hurt

This is a sign that you can start teaching to babies (see page 86), but most won't reproduce it until they are toddlers. It can be very helpful for the nonverbal toddler who needs to let you know his ear hurts. This is a directional sign, so make the sign close to the location of the pain.

Pain

Headache

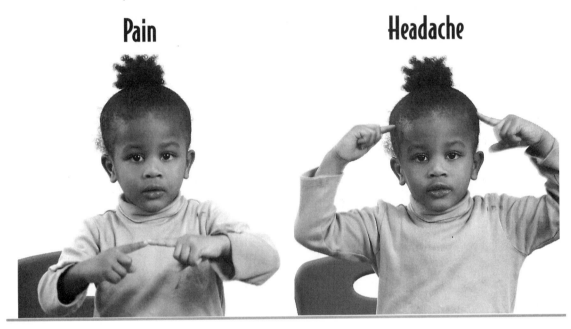

Headache

Touch fingertips together quickly while saying "ouch!"

A good way to teach toddlers the sign for *pain* is to use the rhyme "Five Little Monkeys." Make the sign for *pain* at the end of the second line of the rhyme.

Five Little Monkeys

Five little monkeys jumping on the bed,
One fell off and bumped his head.
(Pause here and say, "Ouch!" as you make the *pain* sign on your head)
Mama called the doctor and the doctor said,
"No more monkeys jumping on the bed!"
(Repeat the rhyme with four little monkeys, then three, and so on.)

Key signs for this song:
Monkey, see page 152
Bed, see page 78
Mama, see page 18
No, see page 51
More, see pages 43 and 69

Snack and Meal Time Signs

Review Chapter 3 for snack and meal time signs. This is the perfect time to reinforce *more*, *please*, *thank you*, and *all done*.

Apple

Toddlers usually point their finger near their cheek or they make a round apple with their fist near the cheek.

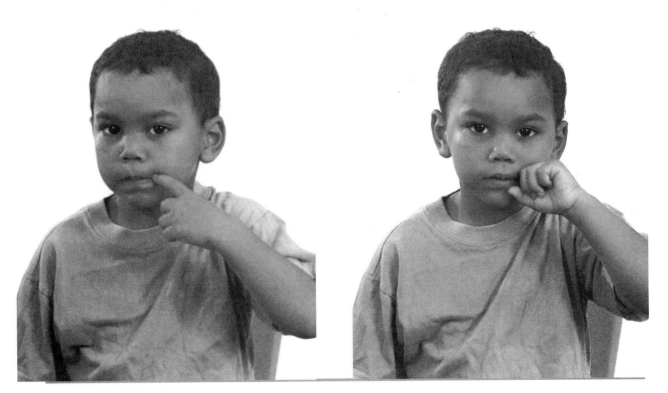

Toddler Sign for Apple

Apple

Twist the knuckle of the forefinger by the side of the mouth or cheek. Imagine your fist being the apple and your bent knuckle the stem of the apple.

Other Meal-Time Signs

More, see page 43   **All Done**, see page 44   **Hungry**, see page 146

Please, see page 26   **Milk**, see page 75   **Thirsty**, see page 146

Thank you, see page 25   **I like it**, see page 146

Banana

Hold up one finger like a banana while the other hand mimics peeling the banana.

Cookie

Indicate the shape of a cookie with one hand pretending to use a cookie cutter in the other hand.

Juice

Form the letter *J* to indicate juice and then make the sign for *drink* as your hand forms a cup that you mimic drinking from.

Cracker

Make a motion with your hand tapping on your elbow to indicate breaking a cracker.

Signs for Clothing

Playing with clothes and dressing up are fascinating activities for toddlers. Shoes and hats hold special interest! Signs for clothes are fun to practice while singing the traditional song, "Mary Wore Her Red Dress." Sing about the children's clothes, substituting their names for Mary's. Also use clothing signs during transitions. For example, sign, "It's time to get your coat." (see page 113).

Mary Wore Her Red Dress

Mary wore her red dress,
Red dress, red dress,
Mary wore her red dress
All day long.

(Sing the song again, replacing "dress" with "hat,""shoes,""pants," and "shirt.")

Dress

Stroke thumbs downward on chest with fingers spread out to indicate clothing.

Hat

Pat your head to represent a hat.

Shoes

Tap closed fists together a few times.

Socks   Shirt

Rub two index fingers side by side.   Tug on your shirt near your shoulder.

Pants

Toddlers will tug on their pants to make this sign.

Hands start on your pants and move upwards as if pulling your pants up to your waistline.

Coat

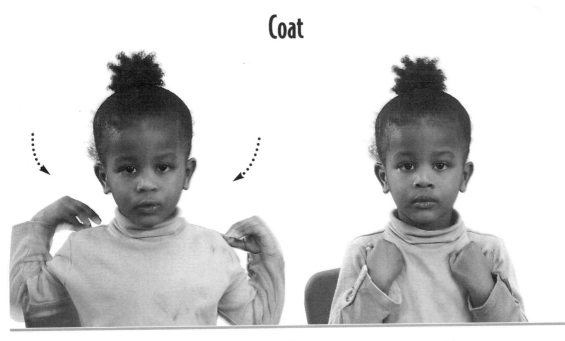

Use both hands and imagine pulling a coat over your shoulders.

Repetitive Physical Games

Because toddlers love to move, physical games are perfect times to reinforce the signs *more* and *all done* (see Chapter 3). For toddlers, you might also want to include the sign *again*. Toddlers seem to like nothing more than doing something again and again! When toddlers engage in physical activities, such as going down a slide over and over again, riding in a swing, playing chase, or playing "Ring Around the Rosie," they will naturally say, "More!" and "Again!"

Again

Touch the fingertips of one hand on the palm of the other hand.

Action Signs

Stand

Stand two fingers in palm of the other hand.

Jump

Show jumping action with two fingers jumping in palm of the other hand.

Note: To sign *dance*, stand two fingers in the palm of other hand and them make the two fingers sway back and forth as if they are legs dancing.

Swing

Sit two fingers of one hand on two fingers of the other hand (the swing) and move the hands back and forth as if swinging.

Slide

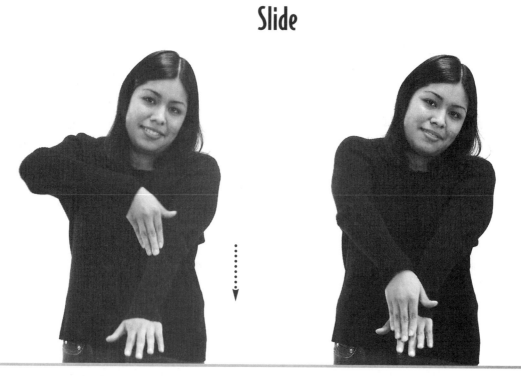

Start one hand near the shoulder of the other arm and slide down the arm.

Teeter Totter

More Action Signs

Sit, see page 41

Stop, see page 31

Go, see page 31

Walk, see page 40

Line up, see page 40

Slightly bend two fingers of each hand with knuckles facing each other. Alternate hands up and down like a teeter totter.

Storybook Signs

Brown Bear, Brown Bear, What Do You See? by Bill Martin Jr. and Eric Carle is a great book to sign because children love learning animal signs. For toddlers, just focus on signing the animals (if you want to add colors, see Chapter 5). Make the signs on the big bold pictures in the book, or use a felt board to retell the story (thus freeing your hands from turning pages while you sign). Also, see chapter 3 for other favorites, including *Goodnight Moon* by Margaret Wise Brown on pages 93–95 and *The Three Bears* on page 137.

Story Time

Make the *F* handshape and interlock both hands.

Break hands apart and move away from one another as if to link several sentences together.

Time

Point to your wrist as if checking the time on your watch.

Brown Bear, Brown Bear, What Do You See? by Eric Carle and Bill Martin, Jr.

Bear Cross your hands and make a claw scratching motion.

Bird Use your thumb and forefinger at your mouth to mimic the action of a bird beak opening and closing.

Duck Use your fingers and thumb to make a duck bill. Open and close fingers in front of your mouth.

Horse With *H* hand, make the ears of the horse.

Frog Flick first two fingers out under the chin as if to show a frog croaking.

Cat Make the whiskers of a cat on your cheek.

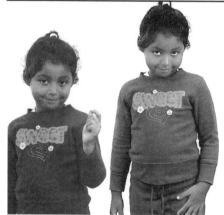

Dog Snap your fingers and pat your leg as if to call a dog.

Sheep Pretend to cut wool of a sheep with the fingers of one hand.

Fish Act out a fish motion with the flat hand "swimming" in front of your body.

Note: See signs for *children* and *teacher* on page 147.

Simple Signing with Young Children

Preposition Signs and Other Early Concepts

A teacher signs *in* while toddlers play.

Many of the signs for animals and actions are iconic (the signs look like the words). This is true of signs for prepositions, which are meaningful concepts for toddlers. Signs such as *on/off* and *in/out* help toddlers see the meaning of the word. *In, out, on,* and *off* are good signs to use because of the frequency with which they are used during repetitive toddler games including stacking blocks, sorting games, and peg boards. See Chapter 5 for preposition signs and other early concepts that can be reinforced with sign language.

Other Signs

Prepositions, see page 157

Colors, see pages 148–149

Seasons, see page 150

Animals, see pages 151–152

Weather, see pages 153–154

Nature, see pages 155–156

Letter to Families

Dear Families:

We are currently using some American Sign Language (ASL) signs for key vocabulary words in the classroom as we work and play together each day. Here are some of the ways we use signs with the toddlers in our program:

We use signs while coaching toddlers to learn social skills:
Although the toddlers are learning how to talk, when they are tired or frustrated it is difficult for them to retrieve the words they want to use. To alleviate this, we encourage toddlers to express themselves with their hands. We show them how to use signs to say things like "Stop," "No," and "Mine." Using signs helps reduce a toddler's frustration, especially in social situations. Using signs also helps keep their hands busy and diverts them from pushing or hitting.

We also use signs to accentuate friendly words:
We use signs for words like "please," "thank you," and "sorry." Signs help give special emphasis to these friendly words.

We use signs to express emotions:
We teach toddlers to use signs to express their emotions, such as happiness, sadness, and anger. Feeling strong emotions can confuse and overwhelm toddlers. Healthy early childhood environments accept and encourage expression of the full range of emotions humans feel. Signs help toddlers read the emotions and social cues of others.

ASL is the third most commonly used language in the United States today and the most common form of communication for deaf people in our country. Teachers are finding that ASL provides many benefits to hearing children, and research shows that children who use signs learn to talk earlier, have larger vocabularies, show increased self-esteem, have greater interest in books, and even have higher IQ scores.

If you want to learn more about the benefits of sign language for hearing children, or have any questions about ASL, please let us know.

Sincerely,

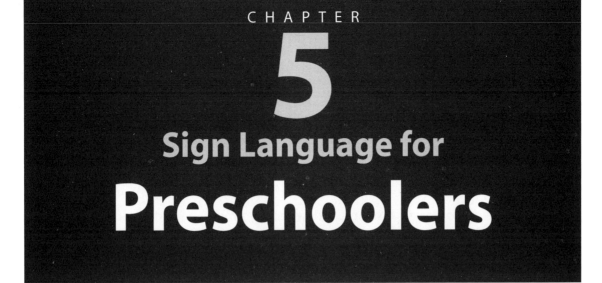

CHAPTER
5
Sign Language for
Preschoolers

A child signs *tree*.

Learning a New Code

Sign language is an expressive communication tool that captivates and engages preschoolers. Preschoolers love seeing and decoding a message with their eyes. Using sign language makes preschoolers feel independent; they feel proud to know how to respond or what to do when they learn signs. Their excitement is similar to the joy and power children experience when they use their first words or when they start to read.

The way you present signs helps bring the novelty and excitement of this new language alive. There are several creative ways to embed signs into the stories, songs, and literacy activities you already use with preschoolers. Just as with babies and toddlers, choose a few signs and start using them without explaining what you are doing. Children enjoy the mystery of figuring out what how to communicate with their hands. Start simply; use the signs for *sit*, *quiet*, and *listen* when the children are gathered at group time (see Chapter 2). If you use these signs quietly and invite children to join once they understand what to do, they will quietly pass the signs on to their peers as they start using the sign along with you. Praise each child for discovering how to listen with her eyes and talk with her hands.

Children and teacher sign *butterfly* while singing a song.

American Sign Language and Deaf Culture

As you learn signs and talk about sign language with preschoolers, you will need to answer questions they have about ASL as well as explain that ASL is a language, the most common language of people who are deaf. Teaching ASL vocabulary to hearing children has the potential of introducing children to another culture, expanding their appreciation and acceptance of a diverse world.

It is important to realize that in the past, people in the hearing community stigmatized deafness. People wrongly considered ASL a primitive communication system. Today's view of deafness recognizes that those who are born deaf may are proud of their identity, and do not need to be "fixed." As with any culture, the language defines its uniqueness. Members of the deaf culture continually advocate for an accurate understanding of ASL as a distinct language with the capacity to express complex ideas and emotions. As more educators and young children enjoy the benefits of ASL, you also promote a respect and appreciation for this beautifully expressive language.

Having children's books available in your class library that illustrate ASL accurately is one of the best ways to present ASL and the deaf culture respectfully to hearing children (see Resources on page 171). Reading these books with children individually and in small and large groups creates opportunities to talk more about ASL as a distinct language.

Keeping a good ASL dictionary on hand is helpful. Also, if you have access to the Internet in your classroom, visit the online dictionary called the ASL Browser at http://commtechlab.msu.edu/sites/aslweb/browser.htm. If you have children or parents who are deaf within your community or if you know other individuals fluent in ASL, they can be wonderful resources to share more information with children about ASL as well. Below are some simple sentences that might be helpful to use in your conversations with young children about ASL and deafness:

- American Sign Language is the most common language used in the United States by people who are deaf.
- Because people who are deaf do not hear, they communicate with their hands.
- American Sign Language is a way to talk with your hands.

- To be good signers, practice moving your hands and holding your hands in special ways to show the words.
- To be good signers, watch closely, look carefully, and learn to listen with your eyes!
- To sign well, use your face to show what you are feeling and thinking.
- Use a dictionary to look up words and phrases, because you are learning about a new language.
- People who are fluent in ASL can say everything they want to say quickly with signs. I don't know how to say everything I'd like to say with sign language because I am still learning.
- Many people who are deaf start learning sign language when they are young, just like you learned how to speak words when you were a baby and toddler.

Literacy and Sign Language

In recent years, researchers discovered a link between using sign language with hearing children and enhanced literacy skills. In her book, *Dancing with Words: Signing for Hearing Children's Literacy*, Dr. Marilyn Daniels documents the benefits of sign language on hearing children's literacy skills, including improved vocabulary scores, spelling proficiency, and reading ability. Because using sign language is a multisensory learning experience, it reinforces children's early literacy development. Sign language and finger spelling are fun and productive ways to actively engage preschoolers in emergent literacy. When you present letters and sounds for children to see, hear, and create with movement, you help build pathways in the brain.

Sign Alphabet Chart

The sign language alphabet is a manual alphabet. Manual alphabet posters are available from parent-teacher stores, but consider making one with
photos of your children doing the signs. Put it on the wall at the children's eye level in the writing center or another appropriate place. Children enjoy standing next to the poster and matching the handshapes with their own hands.

Using the manual alphabet in your classroom helps children make connections about how letters are formed. This connection is similar to the link children make with reading a letter and printing it. Making the sign for a letter can have an even greater effect on children's memory and recognition skills because several of the handshapes for the ASL alphabet look much like the letters they represent, allowing the children to feel the shapes of the letters.

Singing the Alphabet

Depending on the age level and proficiency of your children, consider singing the alphabet while simultaneously signing the manual alphabet during group time. For younger three- and four-year-olds, this can be difficult, while older four- and five-year-olds might be up for the challenge! Try singing and signing the alphabet in a small group, with one or two children gathered around the alphabet poster.

Sky Writing

A fun way for children to feel the shapes of letters is writing letters in the air, or sky writing. Using your hand, write a letter in the air and encourage the children to guess which letter you are making. Then let the children try a similar version of this game, using the many manual alphabet signs that look like the actual letter they represent, such as *Z* or *J*. Children can quickly see the shape of the letter when they form the ASL signs for letters like *C*, *I*, *L*, *O*, *U*, and *W*. Other ASL alphabet signs are great conversation pieces for talking about the shapes that form letters. Some children will be able to make the two humps in the sign for the letter *N* and the three humps in the letter *M*. As children catch on and their symbolic thinking skills become more sophisticated, ask them to explain the more abstract shapes they see in signs for letters like *G* and *P*.

A fun way to link sky writing and the manual alphabet is by writing a letter in the sky, and asking the children to make the signed version of the letter when they know which letter you are making. Let the children take turns writing the letters in the sky while the rest of the class guesses and shows their answer by making the sign for the letter.

The First Letter of Names

A simple way to introduce the manual alphabet is to use the first letter of the children's names as a transition game and tool for dismissing children from group time. As you dismiss the children, say, "If your name starts with this letter (hold up a card with a sign for a manual letter on it or form the sign), you can go wash your hands."

Name Cards

Name cards are a common tool in preschool classrooms. Keep them in a basket in the writing center so that children can use them as a reference to write their own names or the names of their friends. Use name cards as transition tools to dismiss children from group time, or as place markers at the snack table. Also, use name cards to integrate sign language into the classroom by adding a picture of the sign of the first letter of a child's name on the name card, or add a picture of the child making the sign.

Use name cards in the writing center or to label children's cubbies.

Manual Alphabet

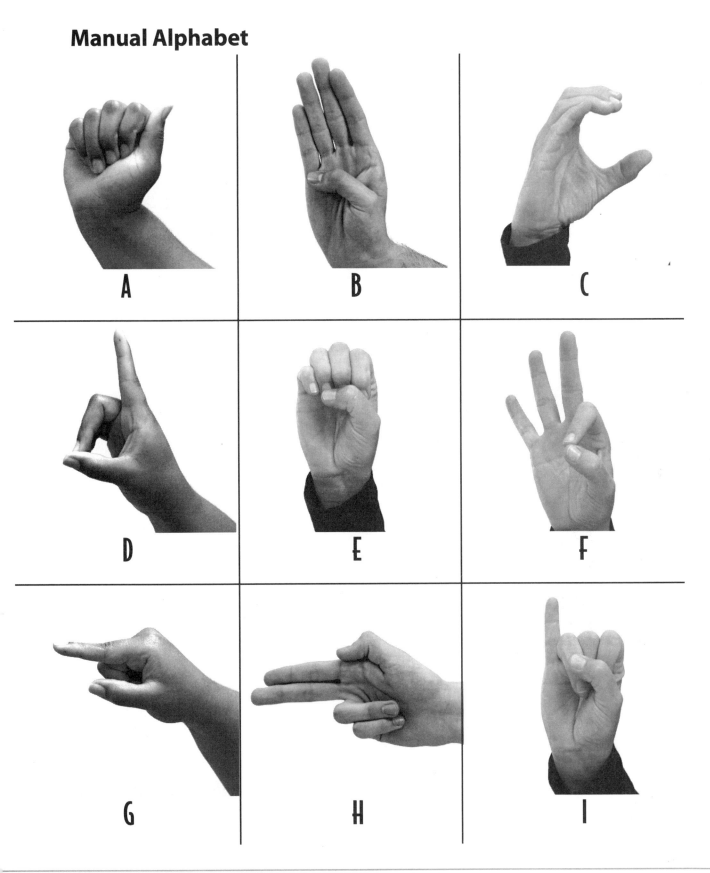

A

B

C

D

E

F

G

H

I

Manual Alphabet

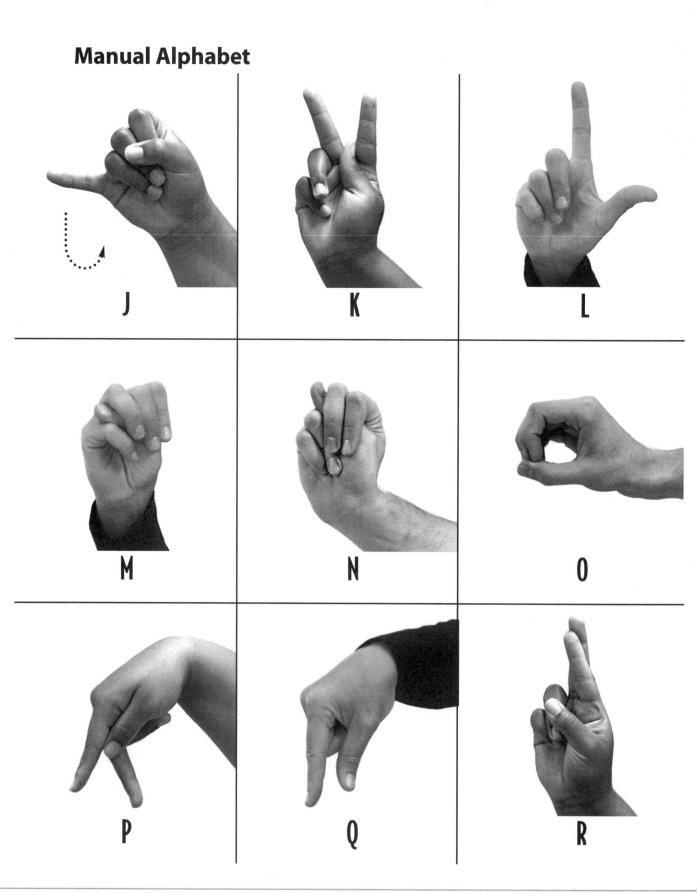

J   K   L

M   N   O

P   Q   R

Manual Alphabet

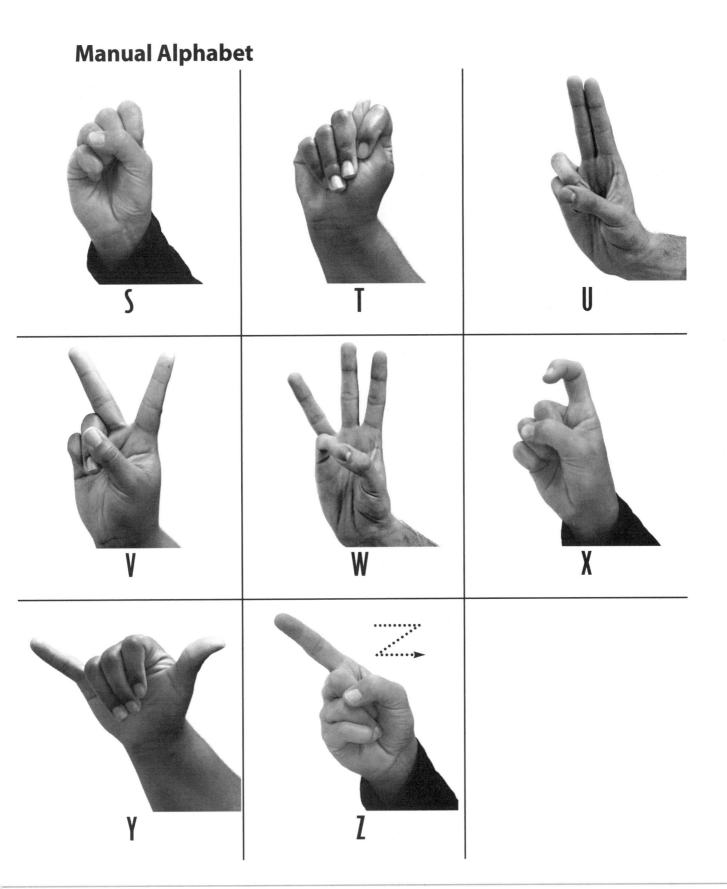

S   T   U

V   W   X

Y   Z

Phonemic Awareness Games

In your classroom, you probably use several songs and poems that use changing letters and sounds to help children hear beginning letter sounds, parts of words, and rhymes. As you use the manual alphabet in your classroom, look for ways to incorporate signing into these songs, games, and poems, such as the samples below.

Fee Fi Fiddle
Tune: "I've Been Working on the Railroad"

Hold up the manual alphabet chart and sing this song with the children. Encourage the children make the manual signs of the letters they want to use in each new verse of the song.

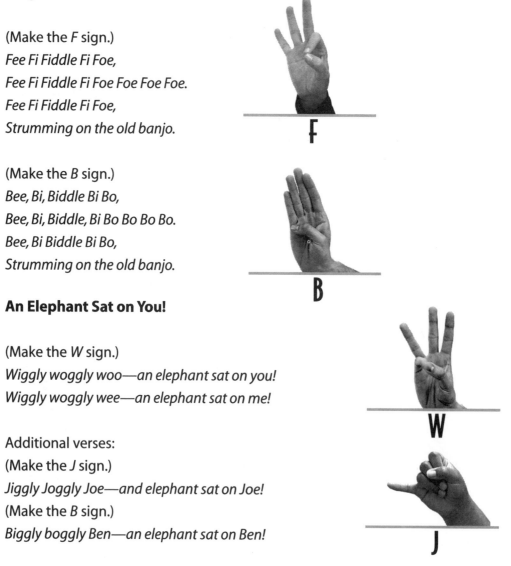

(Make the *F* sign.)
Fee Fi Fiddle Fi Foe,
Fee Fi Fiddle Fi Foe Foe Foe Foe.
Fee Fi Fiddle Fi Foe,
Strumming on the old banjo.

(Make the *B* sign.)
Bee, Bi, Biddle Bi Bo,
Bee, Bi, Biddle, Bi Bo Bo Bo Bo.
Bee, Bi Biddle Bi Bo,
Strumming on the old banjo.

An Elephant Sat on You!

(Make the *W* sign.)
Wiggly woggly woo—an elephant sat on you!
Wiggly woggly wee—an elephant sat on me!

Additional verses:
(Make the *J* sign.)
Jiggly Joggly Joe—and elephant sat on Joe!
(Make the *B* sign.)
Biggly boggly Ben—an elephant sat on Ben!

Fingerplays and Songs

Adding rhythm and music into language exercises taps into yet another mode of learning. There's nothing like melody or rhythm to spark a child's interest and memory. The following are a few traditional songs and fingerplays you can use with a sign vocabulary.

Grandma's Glasses

Here are Grandma's glasses.
Here is Grandma's hat.
This is the way she folds her
hands and puts them in
her lap.

Here are Grandpa's glasses.
Here is Grandpa's hat.
This is the way he folds his
arms, just like that!

Grandma

Sign for *mother* is bumped outward in an arc from the chin to indicate mother's mother.

Grandpa

Sign for *father* is bumped outward from the forehead in an arc to indicate father's father.

Glasses

Indicate the outline of glasses near the top of your eyebrow with first finger and thumb.

Many children prefer to make glasses with their hands for this poem. This is actually the ASL sign for *owl*.

Hat

Touch the top of your head as if to show a hat.

The More We Get Together

The more we get together, together, together,
The more we get together
The happier we'll be.
'Cause your friends are my friends
And my friends are your friends.
The more we get together
The happier we'll be.

More Bring hands together and tap fingertips lightly as if to indicate adding more.

Together Bring hands together and touch fists together in a circle to represent a gathering.

Happy Pat your chest and move in circular motions with flat hands. Imagine happy feelings bubbling up.

Your Extend flat hands outward.

Friends Bring index fingers together and interlock them several times.

My Touch chest.

Skidamarink

Skidamarink a dink a dink,
Skidamarink a doo,
I love you! (Repeat)
I love you in the morning and
in the afternoon.
I love you in the evening
and underneath the
moon!
So, skidamarink a dink a dink,
Skidamarink a doo,
I love you!

I love you

I

Hold up pinky finger.

Love

Hug yourself to indicate *love*.

You

Point towards a person to indicate *you*.

For morning, afternoon, and evening, the horizontal arm represents the earth, while the hand that moves represents the sun. The movement of the hand shows the sun rising and setting.

Morning

Extend your arm and bring it forward. Imagine the sun rising.

Afternoon

Imagine the sun past noon.

Evening/Night

Imagine the sun falling below the horizon.

Note: Horizontal arm represents the horizon. Vertical arm represents the sun rising and setting. One full motion from morning to noon to night represents a day.

Under

Moon

Move one hand under the other hand.

Form a crescent shape with a *C* hand.

Creative Story Telling

A great time to use signs in preschool classrooms is during creative story telling. The best stories to tell aloud are those that are cumulative. Classics like "The Enormous Turnip" have refrains such as, "They pulled and they pulled and they pulled...." Learn the signs to the refrains of the stories you tell, and sign them as you tell the stories. Because they repeat throughout the stories, the children will likely pick up on them and by the end be performing them along with you. Practice using the signs for *mommy, daddy, baby,* and *bear* when telling "The Three Bears." If you don't already have your own version to tell, *The Three Bears* by Byron Barton is an excellent version.

Mommy

Daddy

Baby

Bear

Signing Emotions

Review Chapter 2 for emotion signs. Encourage the children to use emotion signs to facilitate social exchanges and express themselves. Sing "If You're Happy and You Know It" with the children, introducing them to the different signs for the emotions in the song. Preschoolers often want to move beyond the simple signs for *happy* and *sad*, and to learn how to express emotions that are more complex. Below are several examples of simple and more complex emotions.

Excited With both index fingers, strike the heart area and move in small circles.

Proud Move the thumb of one hand up your chest to show chest being puffed up.

Embarrassed Put both hands up to your cheeks as if to show color rising. Expression as if hiding.

Funny Use an *H* handshape to tap the end of your nose.

Silly Wiggle a *Y* handshape in front of your face, almost touching your nose.

Brave Claw hands start open facing chest and then claw hands close quickly as if grabbing strength.

Sad Move outspread fingers down in front of face to show features drooping.

Happy Tap your chest with flat hands or hands in a repeated circular motion. Imagine happiness bubbling up.

Angry Move your clawed hand or hands upwards from your chest to your face. Imagine anger rising.

Scared Hold both hands in front of body near shoulders with fingers closed. Then quickly move hands in front of your chest while fingers spread apart.

Note: You will notice slight variations in the way signs are produced in different ASL dictionaries. Many dictionaries show emotions with one hand while others show using both hands in symmetry (such as with *happy* and *sad*). Both ways are correct. The key is to really show emotion in your facial expressions.

Center and Learning Area Labels

Consider labeling areas or learning centers in your classroom with appropriate manual alphabet signs, so the children can identify them by the signs. If you make your own signs, use photos of the children doing the signs for each center or area.

Art Use your pinky like a paintbrush on the other palm.

Blocks Use a bent hand to touch your other wrist, then repeat with the other hand.

Kitchen Flip a *K* handshape over on your palm as if flipping a pancake.

Library Make small circular movements with an *L* handshape.

Music Swipe your hand up and down your arm rhythmically.

Toilet Make a *T* handshape and shake hand slightly.

Books Open and close your hands as if opening a book.

Writing "Write" on your hand as if holding a pen and writing on paper.

Daily Schedule Signs

If you post a schedule in the classroom, you might also try using ASL-based schedules as visual organizers for children who rely upon predictability. If you create a schedule with magnets or Velcro, you can adjust and change it for specific days as needed.

Snack Mimic pinching food from flat hand. Then mimic eating food with pinched fingers.

Clean Up One hand mimics cleaning the surface of the other hand.

Outside Pull flat hand out of other hand.

Nap/Rest Make the sign for bed by resting your head in your hand.

Play Pivot *Y* handshapes at the wrists.

Lunch (*noon + eat*) Horizontal arm is earth. Vertical arm is noon. Then touch fingers to lips.

Wash Hands Form an *A* handshape with one hand and move it in circular motions over the other hand as if scrubbing or washing.

Integrating Signs into Your Curriculum

Depending on your goals, schedule, classroom routines, and games, you may discover meaningful ways to incorporate the following signs into your classroom.

Group Time Signs

Group Touch hands shapes and then move them as if forming a circle.
Back of hands touch again to close the circle.

Family Make the *group* sign with *F* handshapes.

Class Make the *group* sign with *C* handshapes.

Snack and Meal Time Signs

Meal time is the perfect time to use the signs *more, finished, thank you,* and *please.* You'll find more snack and meal time signs in Chapter 4. Preschoolers enjoy using the signs for *I like it* and *I don't like it*.

Please Place flat hand on chest with fingers closed. Move hand in a circular motion.

More Tap fingers together repeatedly.

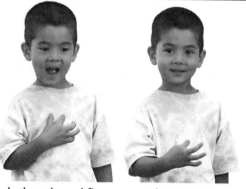

I like it Pinch thumb and finger together near chest. Draw pinched fingers outward (think of drawing out from the heart).

I don't like it Start by showing the *like it* sign, and then push hand away to indicate *don't like.*

Hungry Move your hand in a C shape down your throat and chest to stomach to indicate your desire for food.

Thirsty Move your finger down your throat.

More Meal Time Signs

People Signs

Boy Use a bent hand near your forehead to mimic touching the brim of a hat.

Children With flat hands, palms face down and lightly bounce as if tapping children on their heads.

Girl With *A* hand, stroke one side of your cheek near your chin.

Person Make *P* handshape and move it alongside your body as if to outline a person.

Teacher Combine the signs for *knowledge* and *person*. Touch your forehead and then make *person* sign.

Other People Signs

Color Signs

Try adding color signs to *Brown Bear, Brown Bear, What Do You See?* on page 118. You can also use color signs for transitional games. Ask children to identify the colors that you sign, or try combining colors with clothing signs (see page 110) for "Mary Wore Her Red Dress." Experiment with other verses, such as "blue socks," "white shoes," and so on.

Red Brush your index finger down your lips.

Orange Open and close your hand in front of your mouth, as if squeezing an orange.

Yellow Shake *Y* handshape.

Green Shake *G* handshape.

Blue Shake *B* handshape.

Purple Shake *P* handshape.

Pink Make the *red* sign with the *P* handshape as your middle finger and then your index finger passes near or slightly touch your lips.

Brown Move *B* handshape down your cheek.

Black Move your index finger across your forehead.

White Place an open *five* handshape on your chest and move it out while bringing fingers together.

Note: To use correct ASL grammar in a sign language sentence, the noun comes before the adjective. For example, sock–blue, hat–red, shoe–white.

Season Signs

Winter Hunch your shoulders and clench your fists as if you are cold.

Spring Pass one hand through your other hand to represent plants growing.

Summer Wipe your index finger across your forehead with finger slightly bent.

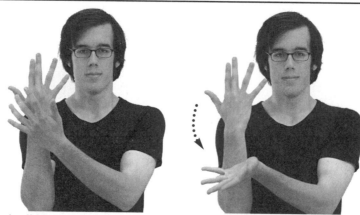

Fall Stand one hand tall like a tree while using the other hand to show leaves falling from the tree.
Note: This is not an ASL sign. It has been adapted for young children.

Animal Signs

For additional animal signs, see *Brown Bear, Brown Bear, What Do You See?* in Chapter 4.

Turtle Form shell with one hand while the other hand forms turtle head peeking out.

Elephant Extend your C hand from your nose like an elephant's trunk.

Giraffe Extend your hand upward from your neck to show a long giraffe neck.

Gorilla Beat your chest like a gorilla.

Other Animal Signs

Owl, see page 132

Mouse, see page 94

Fish, see page 118

Cow, see page 95

Cat, see page 118

Bird, see page 118

Lion Sweep your open-clawed hand over head to indicate a lion's mane.

Snake Place your fingers in a *V* shape to represent fangs. Move your arms in a wavy fashion.

Butterfly Lock thumbs to show shape and movement of butterfly.

Monkey Hunch shoulders and scratch sides to mimic a monkey.

Weather Signs

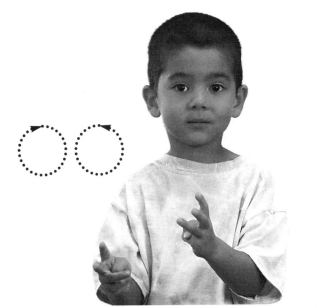

Weather Make *W* handshapes that face each other and move hands in circles.

Clouds Place clawed hands above and beneath each other to form an outline of fluffy clouds.

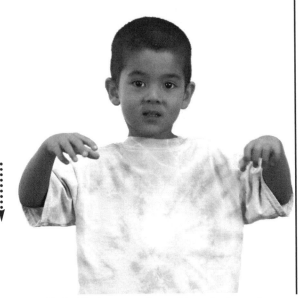

Rain Shake your clawed hands down to mimic rain falling.

Sunny With your finger, draw a circle (*sun*) in the sky.

Windy Bend arms at elbows to show wind blowing. Arms sway back and forth.

Snow There are two acceptable ways to represent *snow* in ASL. One is to wiggle your fingers as they slowly move down in front of your chest to mimic snow falling. Another is to combine the signs for *rain* and *white*.

Nature Signs

Flower Mimic smelling a flower with your fingertips pinched together.

Grass (Note: The ASL sign for *grass* is *green + grow.*)

Moon Make a *C* handshape to form a crescent.

Sky Sweep your hand overhead to show sky.

Star Starting at chest level, rub your index fingers against each other and move upward. Imagine shooting stars.

Tree Your horizontal arm is the earth and your vertical arm is the tree standing with open branches.

Preposition Signs

Up

Point up.

Down

Point down.

In

Put one hand in the other hand as if to put in a container.

Out

Pull one hand out of the other hand as if to pull it out of a container.

On

Move one hand on top of the other hand.

Off

Move one hand off the other hand.

Letter to Families

Dear Families,

We are enjoying using ASL (American Sign Language) in the preschool classroom. Sign language is very motivating to young children because it taps into their desire to learn through movement.

Sign language is a fun way to learn names, shapes, and sounds of alphabet letters. Research shows that sign language promotes early literacy skills. When we sign key words in songs, stories, and games, children can see, feel, and hear language. Children are proud to learn a new language by listening with their eyes and talking with their hands.

Sign language helps create a peaceful classroom. We can give children directions from across the room without having to raise our voices. This promotes each child's sense of pride and independence. There are many benefits to learning a sign vocabulary with young children. We know your child will be proud to show you what he or she is learning.

Sincerely,

Sign Language for an
Inclusive Classroom

A four-year-old practices the sign for *black*.

Approaches for Children with Special Needs

The common theme throughout this book is improving communication between you and the children you teach. One of the great things about using signs with young children is that it gives you another technique to reach children who might otherwise be on the perimeters of the learning circle. This chapter addresses several special approaches that go hand in hand with sign language and that can fit into a developmentally appropriate inclusive program for young children. These approaches are appropriate in special education and integrated settings for children between the ages of two to seven with a range of learning challenges.

Developmentally Appropriate Practice and Special Education

Developmentally appropriate practice and special education approaches can complement one another beautifully. When teachers use developmentally appropriate practices, they prepare open-ended activities, knowing that for younger children, the lesson is in the process. Open-ended activities without prescribed outcomes allow children with special needs who may be functioning at varying developmental levels to work successfully alongside their typically developing peers. Developmental practice also includes opportunities for hands-on learning, sensory play, and movement—just the type of experiences that optimize learning for young children with special needs. Best practices in the field of early childhood education can also be best practices for children with special needs.

Working with Specialists

While using sign language with children with special needs, you should consult and collaborate with a speech and language therapist. Children will do best when teachers and therapists develop an integrated approach. Sign language is one tool that can support a child's success in a group setting and many children will require additional supports based on their language and social needs.

Adaptations and Modifications

The strategies you use for special education purposes can add richness to the classroom that benefits all children. When you adapt your program to meet the needs of children who learn differently, you almost always improve the program for everyone. Early childhood is often the period of life when learning difficulties first become identifiable, so having access to a variety of approaches makes you a better teacher.

Look

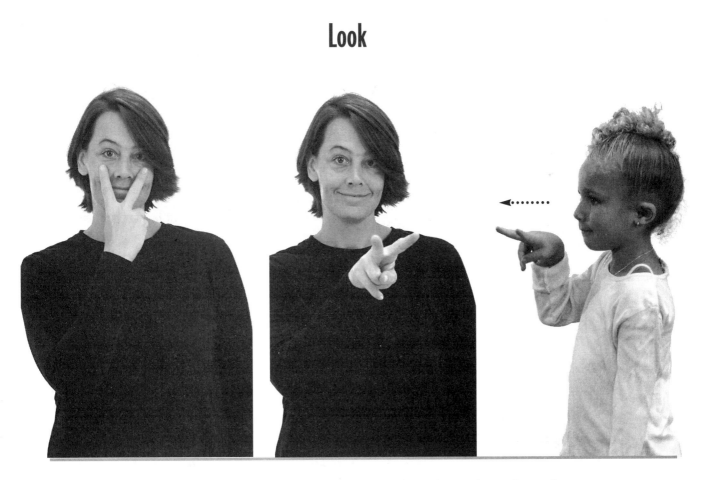

V shape represents eyes looking. Move the V shape forward to indicate the direction the eyes are looking.

Visuals

Visuals help all children learn. Some children with special needs have a particularly difficult time with auditory input, especially if they have delayed language or problems processing language. Many children need to see something to learn it. Sign language helps children focus because language is presented visually. Chapter 5 provides ideas for using visuals such as schedules, labels, photos, and name cards along with signs.

Noise Reduction

Again, because of language processing issues or attention and organizational issues, too much noise can distract or overstimulate children. By using signs, you can give directions without speaking at all. Chapter 2 provides many ideas for using signs to organize transitions, which can be particularly loud and busy times of the day.

Focus

Move flat hands along side of face as if wearing blinders. End this sign by bringing hands together in front of your face to show the focus point.

Eye Contact

Getting and maintaining eye contact with children with special needs can sometimes prove difficult. As you create most signs right in front of your body and near your face, they provide another way to draw a child's attention in your direction. Once children know you are signing, they will be more likely to look up at you. It is a helpful way to get all eyes on you.

Social Coaching

Some children find social interaction difficult and have a hard time reading subtle cues (facial expressions). Signs can teach, reflect, and validate emotions during social coaching. See Chapter 2 for more information.

Multisensory Learning

The idea of using visuals overlaps with multisensory learning. Engaging all our senses helps us make connections. You already know this because when you create developmentally appropriate classrooms, you always include the opportunity to touch, move, look, listen, and sometimes taste! When you teach children to use signs, you integrate several modes of learning. Sign language gives words movement and gives children something purposeful to do with their hands. Many young children need something to touch and hold onto as they learn. Some children use signs as a memory device when trying to remember names of letters in the alphabet. They form the letter with their hand, look at them as if working to recall their names, and then proudly label them.

My

Child produces the sign for *my* by touching chest.

Other Social Signs

Yours, see page 29
Share, see page 27
Friend, see page 27
Emotions, see page 138
Stop, see page 31
Help, see page 29

Kinesthetic learners can *feel* sign language.

Warnings and Preparations

There are many children with special needs who rely heavily upon routine and sameness. Transitions can be challenging for all children, but this is especially true for children with special needs. Signs can add predictability to your routines by signaling that a change is coming. See Chapter 2 for the "Two More Minutes" song and the signs for *one more minute*.

First/Then Strategy

The first/then strategy is appropriate for children who need help getting organized. Sometimes external support such as visuals or picture schedules help to organize a child, because knowing what comes next gives him security. The first/then approach works on the same premise and is helpful for children who have difficulty moving through transitions. When trying this technique, use language sparingly. Too much verbal explanation can overwhelm the children.

Children usually prefer some activities to others, and the first/then strategy helps children who don't want to do a certain activity see that when they complete the activity they don't enjoy, they gain the preferred activity as a reward.

Try using the *then* sign when using the first/then strategy. When telling the child what comes first, touch your thumb. When telling the child what comes next, touch your index finger. This sign serves as a visual organizational tool. "*First* we clean up toys, *then* we have snack." "*First* we put on our coats, *then* we go outside." "*First* we brush our teeth, *then* we read a story."

First

Hold up your index finger and turn it slightly.

Then

With your forefinger, touch your thumb and then the index finger
of your other hand.

Wait Time

Some children may just need a little more time to retrieve language and answer questions appropriately. Building in wait time is good practice for typically developing children too, because all children process and respond at different rates. Children with attention issues sometimes respond too quickly and often inappropriately, so wait time is just another technique to help teach patience. With signs, you can build in the use of a few signs like *wait* and *thinking*. Teach waiting and turn taking during small- and large-group discussions.

Wait   Thinking

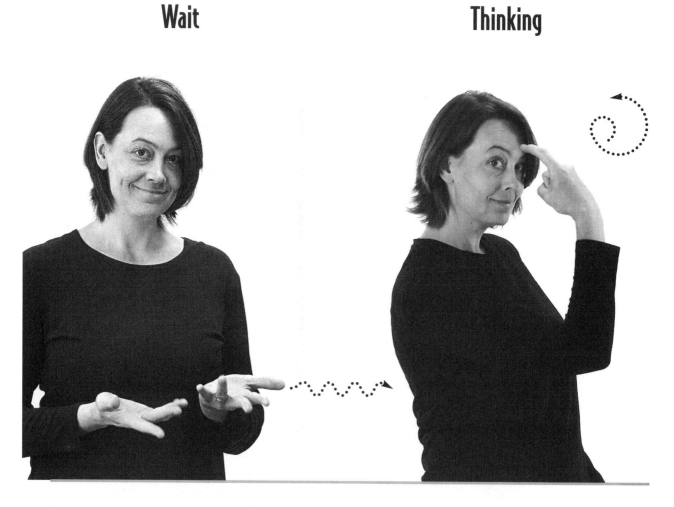

With palms up, wiggle the fingers of both your hands.

Touch the middle of your forehead with your index finger. Move your finger in small circles in front of your forehead to indicate gears turning.

Prompts

Prompts are just reminders or cues to help organize or jump start a child's thinking process. Signs can work very well for prompts. If you are prompting children to use appropriate social language, sign language is a gentle way to remind children of words like "please" and "thank you."

If you are telling a story, and you want a child to recall a key word, you can use signs as a prompt. Simply pause, use the sign as a cue (prompt), and wait for the child to say the word.

Here's an example of how to use signs to prompt children to speak and be involved in an early literacy experience while telling a familiar story.

I see a _____ (pause and sign *horse* as a prompt, wait for the child to say the word, and then continue the story).

Teacher shows the sign *horse* as a prompt, pauses, and waits for the child to fill in the blank.

Hold up your *H* fingers on top of your head to represent horse ears.

Least-to-Most Prompting

Least-to-most prompting is based on the idea of promoting independence by reducing the number of prompts a child needs to be successful. This technique overlaps with the general notion of using prompts to give children cues about what you expect of them. One of the ways to apply this strategy in inclusive early childhood settings is to think of many different ways to deliver a message. If you have to say something more than once, the message might not be coming across and it might be best to communicate the message in another way. Rather than repeat yourself, you could point or whisper or use a sign. The idea is to be supportive but to intrude as little as possible. It is typical in early childhood classrooms for adults to repeat the same message over and over again: "It's time to put your coat on.… Go get your coat.… It's time to get your coat." Reducing verbal prompts by using other means to communicate helps us be patient, less intrusive, and, most importantly, allows children to become more independent.

Total Communication

When you accept and value all the ways to communicate—talking, pointing, signing, mouthing, writing, making facial expressions, gesturing, and using body movement—you value total communication. You must be flexible and allow for many modes of communication when you work with children with special needs. Signs are a supportive strategy, but no strategy is magic. It is always important to individualize your communication strategies as you get to know children. Effective teachers modulate their voices and use facial expressions, gestures, and touch to communicate. Signs are another tool for communicating. They bring a deeper appreciation to the various modes of you have available for connecting with the children and for the children to connect with each other.

Signs as a Bridge to Other Languages

Part of creating an inclusive classroom often includes making learning accessible to children who speak other languages. When I was teaching a small group of autistic boys in Boston, I used signs consistently within our routine for classroom management words and phrases such as *stop, look, listen, group time, sit, please,* and *thank you.* Two of the little boys (one from Morocco and the other from Japan) were not only diagnosed with autism but spoke other languages at home, making their experience in the classroom even more challenging. The basic sign vocabulary I used became an invaluable tool and helped us create our own common language within our classroom community.

Sun

Child uses finger to draw a circle in the sky.

Reflect and Evaluate

As you teach all children, including children with special needs, it is important to evaluate your approaches and the children's responsiveness. You will find that some children are more receptive to signs while others respond better to pictures or variations in voice volume, such as whispering. Sensitive teachers will naturally adapt their approaches to meet the learning styles of children in their care. I hope that sign language will be another communication tool for you and your children.

References and Resources

References

Acredolo, L., S. Goodwyn, and D. Abrams. 2002. *Baby signs: How to talk with your baby before your baby can talk*, revised ed. Chicago, IL: McGraw-Hill/Contemporary Books.

Azpiri, T., and K. Dennis. 2005. *Sign to learn: American Sign Language in the early childhood classroom.* St. Paul, MN: Redleaf Press.

Barton, B. 1999. *The three bears.* New York: HarperCollins.

Bredekamp, S., and C. Copple (Eds.). 1997. *Developmentally appropriate practice in early childhood programs.* Washington, DC: NAEYC.

Briant, M. 2004. *Baby sign language basics.* San Diego, CA: Hay House.

Bricker, D., and J. J. Cripe. 1992. *An activity-based approach to early intervention.* Baltimore, MD: Paul H. Brookes.

Brown, M. W. 1947. *Goodnight moon.* New York: HarperCollins.

Daniels, M. 2001. *Dancing with words: signing for hearing children's literacy.* Westport, CT: Greenwood Publishing.

Garcia, J. 2002. *Sign with your baby*, revised ed. Mukilteo, WA: Northlight Communications.

Goodwyn, S., L. Acredolo, and C. Brown. 2000. Impact of symbolic gesturing on early language development. *Journal of Nonverbal Behavior* (24).

Martin Jr., B., and E. Carle. 1992. *Brown bear, brown bear, what do you see?* New York: Henry Holt.

Resources

ASL Dictionaries

Bahan, B. and J. Dannis. 1990. *Signs for me: Basic vocabulary for children, parents and teachers.* San Diego, CA: Dawn Sign Press.

Flodin, M. 2004. *Signing Illustrated, revised edition.* New York: Perigee Books

Gabriel G. 2003. *Talking with Your Hands, Listening with Your Eyes: A Complete Photographic Guide to American Sign Language.* Square One Publishers.

Riekehof, L. 1987. *The Joy of Signing.* Springfield, MO: Gospel Publishing House

On Line ASL Dictionary

The ASL Browser

http://commtechlab.msu.edu/sites/aslweb/browser.htm

©2000 Michigan State University Communication Technology Laboratory.

Children's Books to Use with Sign Language

Brown Bear, Brown Bear, What Do You See? by Bill Martin, Jr. and Eric Carle

   Use this simple classic story for teaching animal signs

Goodnight Moon by Margaret Wise Brown

   A great book for teaching signs of baby's favorite things

Say Please by Virginia Austin

   A fun book to use with toddlers to reinforce signs *please* and *thank you*

The Three Bears by Byron Barton

   Practice telling this story using signs for *mommy, daddy* and *baby bear*

Children's Sign Language Books for the Classroom Library

A Book of Colors: A Baby's First Sign Book by Kim Votry and Curt Waller

   Baby-toddler-preschooler

The Handmade Alphabet by Laura Rankin

   Preschooler

The Handmade Counting Book by Laura Rankin

   Preschooler

Handsigns: A Sign Language Alphabet by Kathleen Fain

   Toddler-preschooler

My First Book of Sign Language by Joan Holub

   Preschooler

My First Signs (Board Book) by Annie Kubler

   Baby-toddler-preschooler

Out for a Walk: A Baby's First Sign Book by Kim Votry and Curt Walker

   Baby-toddler-preschooler

Simple Signs by Cindy Wheeler

   Baby-toddler-preschooler

Twinkle, Twinkle, Little Star Sign and Singalong by Annie Kubler

   Baby-toddler-preschooler

Index of Signs

A
(p. 127)

Afternoon Imagine the sun past afternoon. (p. 135)

Again Touch the fingertips of one hand on the palm of the other hand. (p. 114)

Airplane The shape of your hand represents an airplane flying overhead. The hand is in the I Love You position. (p. 59, 84)

All Done/Finished Start with your palms facing up and then flip your hands outward. Imagine clearing the table. (p. 44, 70)

Angry Move clawed hands up toward your face. Think of rage rising up inside you. (p. 35, 139)

Apple Twist the knuckle of the forefinger by the side of the mouth or cheek. Imagine your fist being the apple and your bent knuckle the stem of the apple. (p. 107)

Apple (child adaptation) (p. 107)

Art Use your pinky like a paintbrush on the other palm. (p. 141)

B (p. 127, 130)

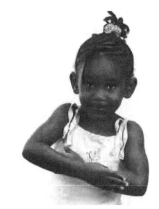

Baby Sway your arms together as if rocking a baby. (p. 82, 137)

Ball Form a ball shape with your fingers, as if grasping a ball with your palms facing. (p. 81)

Balloon Hands begin close to the mouth. Move hands outward as if holding a balloon while blowing it up. (p. 83, 94)

Banana Hold up one finger like a banana while the other hand mimics peeling the banana. (p. 19, 108)

Bear/Bears With arms crossed, use clawed hands to open and close fingers as if to scratch. (p. 95, 118, 137)

Bed Rest your head on your hand. (p. 78)

Bird Form a beak with your hand in front of your lips. Open and close thumb and finger to show a beak opening and closing. (p. 17, 87, 118)

Black Move your index finger across your forehead. (p. 149, 159)

Blanket Pull your hands upward from your waist, as if pulling a blanket up over you and tucking yourself in. (p. 79)

Blocks Use a bent hand to touch your other wrist, then repeat with the other hand. (p. 141)

Blue Shake *B* handshape. (p. 148)

Book/Books Open and close your hands in front of you as if opening a book. (p. 57, 88, 89, 142)

Bottle Imagine you are grasping the bottle with one hand and placing it on the other hand. (p. 75)

Bottle (child adaptation) Use your thumb or finger to symbolize a bottle. Mimic a drinking motion with this adapted sign. (p. 75)

Bowl of Mush Use your hand to mimic eating cereal from a bowl. (p. 95)

Boy Bend your hand at your forehead as if touching the rim of a cap. (p. 55, 147)

Brave Claw hands start open facing chest and then claw hands close quickly as if grabbing strength. (p. 139)

Brown Move *B* handshape down your cheek. (p. 149)

Brush/Hairbrush Mimic holding brush and sweep hand downward as if brushing. (p. 95)

Butterfly Lock thumbs to show shape and movement of butterfly. (p. 122, 152)

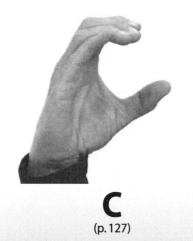

C
(p. 127)

Calm After making the *quiet* sign above, cross your arms and sweep them down in a smooth, graceful motion. (p. 37)

Car/Truck Rotate hands as if driving. (p. 81)

Cat Make the whiskers of a cat on your cheek. (p. 17, 67, 118)

Chairs Show the *sit* sign and repeat it. Sit: place two fingers of one hand on two fingers of your other hand. (p. 95)

Change Rotate fists back and forth as if shifting/changing. (p. 80)

Children With flat hands, palms face down and lightly bounce as if tapping children on their heads. (p. 147)

Choice Use one hand to pick and choose from the fingertips of the other hand. Envision picking berries. (p. 56)

Class Make the *group* sign with *C* handshapes. (p. 145)

Clean Up One hand mimics cleaning the surface of the other hand. (p. 143)

Cleaning Move one hand in a circular motion as if cleaning the surface of the other hand. (p. 38)

Clever/Smart Touch your index finger to your forehead and then move it away from your head as you point forward. Imagine forward thinking. (p. 52)

Clocks Point to your wrist as if looking at the time. (p. 94)

Close/Closed Move flat hands back together. Toddlers may represent this sign by placing their hands flat together and then opening and closing them like a book. (p. 102)

Clouds Place clawed hands above and beneath each other to form an outline of fluffy clouds. (p. 153)

Coat/Coats Imagine pulling a coat over your shoulders. (p. 39, 113)

Cold With closed fists, shiver as if you are cold. (p. 104)

Cookie Indicate the shape of a cookie with one hand pretending to use a cookie cutter in the other hand. (p. 108)

Cows Make an *L* handshape with hands and put them on your head to show horns of a cow. (p. 95)

Cracker Make a motion with your hand tapping on your elbow to indicate breaking a cracker. (p. 109)

Cry With your fingers, show tears rolling down your cheeks. (p. 36)

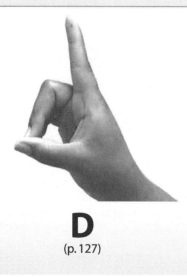

D
(p. 127)

Daddy With an open hand, use your thumb to tap your forehead and wiggle your fingers slightly. (p. 18, 137)

Diaper Hold both hands up as if pinching the corners of a diaper. (p. 80)

Dog Snap your fingers and pat your leg as if to call a dog. (p. 118)

Down Point down. (p. 76, 157)

Dress Stroke thumbs downward on chest with fingers spread out to indicate clothing. (p. 110)

Drink Cup a hand at your mouth and tip your head up as if drinking from a cup. (p. 73)

Duck Use your fingers and thumb to make a duck bill. Open and close fingers in front of your mouth. (p. 118)

E
(p. 127)

Eat Tap your fingertips to lips as if eating. (p. 72, 89)

Elephant Extend your C hand from your nose like an elephant's trunk. (p. 151)

Embarrassed Put both hands up to your cheeks as if to show color rising. Expression as if hiding. (p. 138)

Evening Imagine the sun falling below the horizon.

Excited With both index fingers, strike the heart area and move in small circles. (p. 138)

F

(p. 127, 130)

Family Make the *group* sign with *F* handshapes. (p. 145)

Fall (season) Stand one hand tall like a tree while using the other hand to show leaves falling from the tree. **Note:** This is not an ASL sign. It has been adapted for young children. (p. 150)

Fan Point your index finger up and circle it around to mimic the fan spinning. (p. 83)

Fast Tuck your thumb under your index finger, and then quickly snap it out to show something moving quickly. (p. 33)

Finished/All Done Move open hands outward as if finished with something or pushing something away. (p. 44, 70)

First Hold up your index finger and turn it slightly. (p. 165)

Fish With your fingers together, "swim" your hand in front of you like a fish in water. (p. 87, 118)

Flower Mimic smelling a flower with your fingertips pinched together. (p. 155)

Focus Move flat hands along side of face as if wearing blinders. End this sign by bringing hands together in front of your face to show the focus point. (p. 162)

Friends/Friendship Imagine two people hugging and being close friends. Bring your index fingers together and interlock them several times. (p. 27, 133)

Frog Flick first two fingers out under the chin as if to show a frog croaking. (p. 118)

Funny Use an *H* handshape to tap the end of your nose. (p. 138)

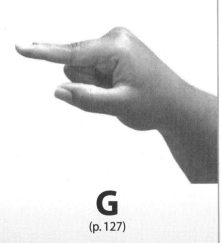

G

(p. 127)

Gentle With palms up, open and close your hands in a gentle way. (p. 28)

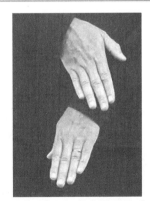

Gentle Touch "One hand pets the other." (p. 28)

Get Reach out your hands as if to get something and bring them to your chest. (p. 39)

Giraffe Extend your hand upward from your neck to show a long giraffe neck. (p. 151)

Girl With an *A* hand, stroke the side of your cheek or chin along the jaw line. (p. 55, 147)

Glasses Indicate the outline of glasses near the top of your eyebrow with first finger and thumb. (p. 132)

Go Point your index fingers and make a swift movement forward as if to indicate, "Go." (p. 31)

Good Start with a flat hand at your lips and move it outward, as if blowing a kiss (this sign means both *good* and *thank you*). (p. 25, 53)

Gorilla Beat your chest like a gorilla. (p. 151)

Grandma Sign for *mother* is bumped outward in an arc from the chin to indicate mother's mother. (p. 131)

Grandpa Sign for *father* is bumped outward from the forehead in an arc to indicate father's father. (p. 131)

Grass (**Note:** The ASL sign for grass is *green + grow.*) (p. 155)

Green Shake *G* handshape. (p. 148)

Group Touch hands shapes and then move them as if forming a circle. Back of hands touch again to close the circle. (p. 145)

H

(p. 127)

Happy Pat your chest and move in circular motions with flat hands. Imagine happy feelings bubbling up. (p. 16, 35, 133, 139)

Hat Pat your head to represent a hat. (p. 111, 132)

Headache Touch fingertips together quickly while saying "ouch!" (p. 105)

Hear/Listen Cup a C handshape around your ear. (p. 90)

Help Rest one fist in the palm of the other hand. Lift hands up together several inches in front of your chest. Imagine one hand "helping" the other hand up. (p. 29)

Horse With *H* hand, make the ears of the horse. (p. 118, 167)

Hot Place a cupped hand to your mouth and quickly draw it away as if your breath is hot. (p. 104)

House Outline the roof of a house with your hands. (p. 94)

Hungry Move your hand in a C shape down your throat and chest to stomach to indicate your desire for food. (p. 146)

I (p. 127, 134)

"I Don't Like It" Start by showing the *like it* sign, and then push hand away to indicate *don't like*. (p. 146)

"I Like It" Pinch thumb and finger together near chest. Draw pinched fingers outward (think of drawing out from the heart). (p. 146)

"I Love You" (p. 134)

Idea Bounce your pinky finger off your forehead, then move your hand up and out from the side of your head. (p. 54)

In Put one hand in the other hand as if to put in a container. (p. 119, 157)

J
(p. 128, 130)

Juice Form the letter *J* to indicate juice and then make the sign for *drink* as your hand forms a cup that you mimic drinking from. (p. 109)

Jump With two fingers of one hand, act out jumping in the palm of your other hand. (p. 95, 115)

K
(p. 128)

Kitchen Flip a *K* handshape over on your palm as if flipping a pancake. (p. 141)

Kittens Smooth out the whiskers of a cat on your cheeks. **Note:** This is the ASL sign for *cat*. Use the sign for *baby* (p. 174) and *cat* to say *kitten*. (p. 94)

Know Touch your fingertips to your forehead. (p. 48)

L
(p. 128)

Index of Signs

Lady Use the thumb of your shaped hand to stroke your cheek near the chin. Tap your chest with the thumb. (p. 95)

Library Make small circular movements with an *L* handshape. (p. 141)

Light With one hand, point closed fingers down, then spread your fingers as if rays of light are shining down. (p. 84, 94)

Line Up Point your fingers up straight (with thumbs tucked in). Start with your hands a few inches apart and move them away from one another to show a line forming. (p. 40)

Lion Sweep your open-clawed hand over head to indicate a lion's mane. (p. 16, 152)

Listen Cup a *C* handshape around your ear. (p. 46, 90)

Look Use a *V* hand to represent the eyes looking forward. (p. 46, 161)

Love A toddler signs *love* by crossing her arms in front of her chest as if to give a hug. (p. 103, 134)

Lunch (*noon + eat*) Horizontal arm is earth. Vertical arm is noon. Then touch fingers to lips. (p. 144)

M
(p. 128)

Milk Open and close your hand repeatedly as if milking a cow. (p. 75)

Minutes Hold one hand flat like the face of a clock. Move the index finger of your other hand in an arc to indicate minutes ticking. (p. 42)

Mittens Mimic action of putting on mittens. (p. 95)

Mommy With an open hand, use your thumb to tap your chin and wiggle your fingers slightly. (p. 18, 137)

Monkey Hunch shoulders and scratch sides to mimic a monkey. (p. 152)

Moon The C handshape represents a crescent-shaped moon. (p. 85, 94, 136, 155)

More Bring your hands together and gently tap your fingers together repeatedly. (p. 42, 43, 69, 71, 100, 133, 146)

More (child adaptation) (p. 66)

Morning (child adaptation) Extend your arm and bring it forward. Imagine the sun rising. (p. 135)

Mouse Brush your index finger on your nose to indicate twitching nose of mouse. (p. 94)

Music Sweep a flat hand up and down the other arm rhythmically. (p. 91, 142)

My Using a flat hand with your fingers together, touch your chest to indicate *my*. (p. 29, 133, 163)

N
(p. 128)

Nap/Rest Make the sign for bed by resting your head in your hand. (p. 144)

Night (child adaptation) Imagine the sun falling below the horizon. (p. 135)

No Snap your thumb and middle finger closed. (p. 51)

O
(p. 128)

Off Move one hand off the other hand. (p. 157)

Old Cup chin with your hand and move downward to show a long beard. (p. 95)

On Move one hand on top of the other hand. (p. 157)

One (p. 15, 43)

Open Move flat hands apart as if opening a window. (p. 9, 102)

Orange Open and close your hand in front of your mouth, as if squeezing an orange. (p. 148)

Out Pull one hand out of the other hand as if to pull it out of a container. (p. 157)

Outside Pull flat hand out of other hand. (p. 144)

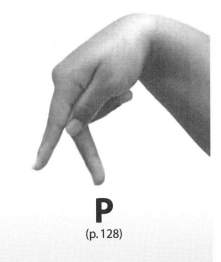

P (p. 128)

Pain Pointer fingers quickly touch each other to indicate pain. If your head hurts, the sign is made on your head. If your knee hurts, the sign is made on your knee. (p. 86, 105)

Pain (Headache) Touch fingertips together quickly while saying "ouch!" (p. 21, 105)

Pants Hands start on your pants and move upwards as if pulling your pants up to your waistline. (p. 113)

Perfect Touch a *P* hand to the other *P* hand. (p. 56)

Person Make *P* handshape and move it alongside your body as if to outline a person. (p. 147)

Pink Make the *red* sign with the *P* handshape as your middle finger and then your index finger passes near or slightly touch your lips. (p. 149)

Play Make the Y handshape with both hands and shake your hands back and forth. (p. 20, 42, 144)

Please Place a flat hand on your chest. Rub chest in a circular motion (as if to warm your heart). (p. 26, 146)

Proud Move the thumb of one hand up your chest to show chest being puffed up. (p. 138)

Purple Shake *P* handshape. (p. 148)

Q
(p. 128)

Quiet Put one finger at your lips. (p. 37)

R
(p. 128)

Rain Shake your clawed hands down to mimic rain falling. (p. 153)

Ready With two *R* hands (cross your first two fingers), point out to one side. Swing your hands from side to side. (p. 47)

Red Brush your index finger down your lips. (p. 148)

Remember Touch your thumb to your forehead, and then touch it to other thumb (as if to know something and to keep it). (p. 50)

Rest/Nap Make the sign for bed by resting your head in your hand. (p. 144)

S
(p. 129)

Sad Move outstretched fingers down your face to represent sad feelings or tears. (p. 34, 139)

Scared Hold both hands in front of body near shoulders with fingers closed. Then quickly move hands in front of your chest while fingers spread apart. (p. 139)

Share Imagine slicing a cake to share with others. The movement of the hand represents dividing things up. Both hands are flat and open with fingers together. (p. 27)

Sheep Pretend to cut wool of a sheep with the fingers of one hand. (p. 118)

Shirt Tug on your shirt near your shoulder. (p. 112)

Shoes Form two shoes with your closed fists and tap them together several times. (p. 20, 111)

Silly Wiggle a *Y* handshape in front of your face, almost touching your nose. (p. 138)

Siren Lift claw handshapes overhead while rotating at the wrists to show lights spinning on top of an ambulance. (p. 92)

Sit Use two fingers of one hand to "sit" on two fingers of the other hand (imagine legs sitting on a bench). (p. 41)

Sky Sweep your hand overhead to show sky. (p. 155)

Sleep Sweep an open hand down over your face and close it near your chin. (p. 77)

Slide Start one hand near the shoulder of the other arm and slide down the arm. (p. 116)

Slow Draw one hand slowly up the back of your other hand. (p. 33)

Smart Touch your middle finger to your forehead. (p. 52)

Snack Mimic pinching food from flat hand. Then mimic eating food with pinched fingers. (p. 143)

Snake Place your fingers in a *V* shape to represent fangs. Move your arms in a wavy fashion. (p. 152)

Snow Wiggle your fingers as they slowly move down in front of your chest to mimic snow falling or combine the signs for *rain* and *white*. (p. 154)

Socks Rub your index fingers back and forth against each other. (p. 94, 112)

Sorry Place an *S* hand on your chest and move it in a circular motion. (p. 26)

Sound Point to your ear. (p. 90)

Spring Pass one hand through your other hand to represent plants growing. (p. 150)

Stand Stand two fingers in palm of the other hand. (p. 115)

Star Starting at chest level, rub your index fingers against each other and move upward. Imagine shooting stars. (p. 156)

Stop Chop down quickly with your action hand into a flat base hand. Imagine something coming to an abrupt stop. (p. 19, 23, 31, 45)

Story Time Make the *F* handshape and interlock both hands. Break hands apart and move away from one another as if to link several sentences together. (p. 117)

Summer Wipe your index finger across your forehead with finger slightly bent. (p. 150)

Sun Child uses finger to draw a circle in the sky. (p. 169)

Sunny With your finger, draw a circle (*sun*) in the sky. (p. 153)

Swing Sit two fingers of one hand on two fingers of the other hand (the swing) and move the hands back and forth as if swinging. (p. 115)

T
(p. 129)

Teacher Combine the signs for *knowledge* and *person*. Touch your forehead and then make *person* sign. (p. 147)

Teeter Totter Slightly bend two fingers of each hand with knuckles facing each other. Alternate hands up and down like a teeter totter. (p. 116)

Telephone Hold your hand up as if talking on the phone. (p. 92, 94)

Thank You/Good Hand starts at lips and moves outward, as if blowing a kiss (this sign means both *good* and *thank you*). (p. 24, 25, 97)

Then With your forefinger, touch your thumb and then the index finger of your other hand. (p. 165)

Index of Signs

Thinking Touch the middle of your forehead with your index finger. Move your finger in small circles in front of your forehead, as though to indicate gears turning. (p. 49, 166)

Thirsty Move your finger down your throat. (p. 146)

Time Point to your wrist as if checking the time on your watch. (p. 38, 43, 117)

Tired Touch your hands to your shoulders, then droop as you hunch shoulders forward. (p. 78)

To Touch your index fingers together. (p. 42)

Together Bring hands together and touch fists together in a circle to represent a gathering. (p. 133)

Toilet Shake a *T* handshape slightly from side to side. (p. 80, 142)

Touch Use middle finger to touch back of other hand. (p. 28)

Train With palms facing down, slide first two fingers of one hand (*U* handshape) forward and back along the first two fingers of the other hand. (p. 82)

Tree Your horizontal arm is the earth and your vertical arm is the tree standing with open branches. (p. 121, 156)

Truck/Car Rotate hands as if driving. (p. 81)

Turtle Form shell with one hand while the other hand forms turtle head peeking out. (p. 151)

Two Hold two fingers up. (p. 42)

U
(p. 129)

Under Move one hand under the other hand. (p. 136)

Up Point up. (p. 76, 157)

V
(p. 129)

W
(p. 129, 130)

Wait/Waiting With palms up, wiggle the fingers of both hands. (p. 48, 166)

Walk Place your flat hands in front of your chest with palms facing down. Move your hands forward alternately as if to symbolize the walking motion of feet. (p. 40)

Want Extend both hands out and then bring them closer into the body while the fingers curl up. Toddlers may simply open and close fingers to show the sign. (p. 101)

Wash Hands Form an *A* handshake with one hand and move it in circular motions over the other hand as if scrubing or washing. (p. 144)

Water Put a *W* hand to your lips. (p. 74)

Weather Make *W* handshapes that face each other and move hands in circles. (p. 153)

White Place an open *five* handshape on your chest and move it out while bringing fingers together. (p. 149)

Wind/Windy Children imagine a windy day as the hands sway back and forth to show the movement of the wind. (p. 19, 150)

Winter Hunch your shoulders and clench your fists as if you are cold. (p. 150)

Work Use one *S* hand to tap the other *S* hand, as though hammering. (p. 53)

Writing "Write" on your hand as if holding a pen and writing on paper. (p. 142)

X

(p. 129)

Y

(p. 129)

Yellow Shake *Y* handshape. (p. 148)

Yes Shake an S hand up and down. Imagine a head nodding, "Yes." (p. 51)

You Point towards a person to indicate you. (p. 134)

Your/Yours Using a flat hand with your fingers together, move your hand forward to indicate *your*. (p. 29, 39, 133)

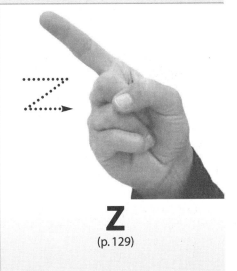

Z

(p. 129)

Index

Reading Games for Young Children

Jackie Silberg

When you bend yourself into a letter shape or have an alphabet phone conversation, learning to read is FUN. Young children learn and retain more information when they are enjoying themselves. In *Reading Games,* best-selling author Jackie Silberg offers more than 200 activities that will keep children ages three to six engaged, interested, and entertained as they acquire the skills they need to become successful readers. Organized by elements of literacy, such as alliteration, alphabet, letter sounds, and rhyming, this book provides research-based information on the importance of literacy development in young children. The fun and easy-to-do activities require little preparation and few materials. 160 pages. 2005.

ISBN 978-0-87659-243-4 | Gryphon House | 16951

Available at your favorite bookstore, school supply store, or order from Gryphon House at 800.638.0928 or www.ghbooks.com

Everyday Literacy

Environmental Print Activities forChildren 3 to 8

Stephanie Mueller

Everyday Literacy has more than 100 activities that use ordinary objects such as cereal boxes, traffic signs, and toy labels to help children build essential reading skills. With games such as "Chalk Chat" and projects like "Alphabet Scrapbooks," children will enjoy learning to recognize the letters, symbols, and words around them. 256 pages. 2005.

ISBN 978-0-87659-286-1 | Gryphon House | 18462

Read! Move! Learn!

Active Stories for Active Learning

Carol Totsky Hammett and Nicki Collins Geigert

Read! Move! Learn! has active learning experiences based on more than 70 children's books. With theme connections, related books and music, lesson objectives, a vocabulary list, a concept list, and a variety of activities, this book will engage young children with hours of exciting literacy lessons! 232 pages. 2007.

ISBN 978-0-87659-058-4 | Gryphon House | 13497

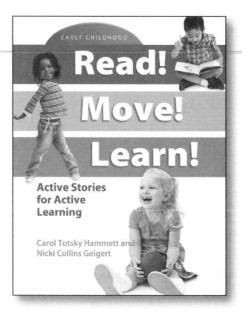

Jump into Literacy

Active Learning for Preschool Children

Rae Pica

Jump into Literacy combines children's love of active games with over 100 lively literacy activities. These joyful games will engage the whole child in moving and playing as a way to develop the literacy skills needed for reading and writing. Each activity is complete with a literacy objective, a materials list, instructions, and extension activities. Most of the activities include suggestions for related music and children's books. 136 pages. 2007.

ISBN 978-0-87659-009-6 | Gryphon House | 15462

Inclusive Lesson Plans Throughout the Year

Laverne Warner, Sharon Lynch, Diana Nabors, and Cynthia Simpson

Inclusive Lesson Plans Throughout the Year has more than 150 lesson plans designed for teachers who need to adapt their classrooms for children with autism; speech, hearing, visual, or orthopedic impairments; ADHD; or learning disabilities. Each lesson plan has a learning objective, a materials list, directions for preparation, an assessment component, extension activities, and a variety of adaptations for children with special needs. 352 pages. 2007.

ISBN 978-0-87659-014-0 | Gryphon House | 18302

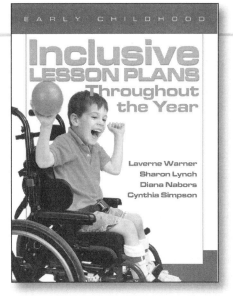

The Inclusive Learning Center Book

For Preschool Children with Special Needs

Christy Isbell and Rebecca Isbell

The Inclusive Learning Center Book is designed for teachers and directors who work with all young children, both those with special needs and those who are developing typically. The activities in each learning center have suggested adaptations that will help these activities be effective for children with special needs. The last two chapters of the book focus on assessment and evaluation tools and building and creating items for centers that will be especially useful for children with special needs. 320 pages. 2005.

ISBN 978-0-87659-014-0 | Gryphon House | 19357